The Apologies

of

Justin Martyr

Translations of

The Rev. Alexander Roberts, DD

And

James Donaldson, LLD

with Brief Notes and Prefaces,

By

A. Cleveland Coxe, DD

Τά άρχαϊα Εθη κραγείγω

A classic reprint by

SUzeteo Enterprises

συζητεο πραγματων

The Apologies

of

Justin Martyr

Translations of

The Rev. Alexander Roberts, DD

And

James Donaldson, LLD

with Brief Notes and Prefaces,

By

A. Cleveland Coxe, DD

Τά άρχαϊα Εθη κραγείγω

A classic reprint by

S zeteo Enterprises

συζητεο πραγματων

The Apologies of Justin Martyr

Translations of Rev. Alexander Roberts, DD and James Donaldson, LLD. Brief notes and prefaces by A. Cleveland Coxe, DD.

This is a reprint, faithfully transcribed, of Justin's *Apologies* found in an edition of *The Ante Nicene Fathers* originally published in 1885 by the Christian Literature Publishing Company.

Soft Cover ISBN: 978-1936830-36-7
Hard Cover ISBN: 978-1-936830-76-3

Published by Suzeteo Enterprises

Cover Design by Julius Broqueza.

FROM THE PUBLISHER

Justin Martyr was one of the earliest contenders for the Christian faith. Like so many other Christians at the time, Justin suffered the ultimate punishment: death. Justin Martyr argued with philosophers, cynics, and skeptics wherever he found them. This included even the Roman Senate, the audience Justin had in mind for the two apologies (or, 'defenses') contained in this volume. Justin sought to set the record straight about what the Christians truly believed in the face of lies, slanders, and misunderstandings that were prevalent throughout the Roman Empire.

There are *still* lies, slanders, and misunderstandings of Christianity. Many of these are still answered by Justin Martyr, though he wrote nearly two thousand years ago. At the very least, an understanding of the controversies of old will shed light on today's controversies. It may head off objections to Christianity before they even begin.

On the other hand, it will certainly surprise many modern readers that in the beginning, some in the Roman Empire regarded Christianity as espousing *atheism*. It does not seem that this particular confusion will arise in the modern mind any time soon. Bearing in mind Justin's unique time and place will help keep his arguments in context. The helpful notes by A. Cleveland Coxe are retained in the hope that they will provide insight into that context.

An up to date index has been created to aid the serious student of Christianity even more. It is our hope that this edition will prove its worth and become a valuable inclusion in any library.

INTRODUCTORY NOTE TO THE
FIRST APOLOGY OF JUSTIN MARTYR

[A.D. 110-165.] JUSTIN was a Gentile, but born in Samaria, near Jacob's well. He must have been well educated: he had travelled extensively, and he seems to have been a person enjoying at least a competence. After trying all other systems, his elevated tastes and refined perceptions made him a disciple of Socrates and Plato. So he climbed towards Christ. As he himself narrates the story of his conversion, it need not be anticipated here. What Plato was feeling after, he found in Jesus of Nazareth. The conversion of such a man marks a new era in the gospel history. The sub-apostolic age begins with the first Christian author,—the founder of theological literature. It introduced to mankind, as the mother of true philosophy, the despised teaching of those Galileans to whom their Master had said, "Ye are the light of the world."

And this is the Epoch which forced this great truth upon the attention of contemplative minds. It was more than a hundred years since the angels had sung "Good-will to men;" and that song had now been heard for successive generations, breaking forth from the lips of sufferers on the cross, among lions, and amid blazing faggots. Here was a nobler Stoicism that needed interpretation. Not only choice spirits, despising the herd and boasting of a loftier intellectual sphere, were its professors; but thousands of men, women, and children, withdrawing themselves not at all from the ordinary and humble lot of the people, were inspired by it to live and die heroically and sublimely,—exhibiting a superiority to revenge and hate entirely unaccountable, praying for their enemies, and seeking to glorify their God by love to their fellow-men.

And in spite of Gallios and Neros alike, the gospel was dispelling the gross darkness. Of this, Pliny's letter to Trajan is decisive evidence. Even in Seneca we detect reflections of the daybreak. Plutarch writes as never a Gentile could have written until now. Plato is practically surpassed by him in his thoughts upon the "delays[1] of the Divine Justice." Hadrian's address to his soul, in his dying moments, is a tribute to the new ideas which had been sown in the popular mind. And now the Antonines, impelled by something in the age, came forward to reign as "philosophers." At this moment, Justin Martyr confronts them like a Daniel. The "little stone" smites the imperial image in the face, not yet "in the toes." He tells the professional philosophers on a throne how false and hollow is all wisdom that is not meant for all humanity, and that is not capable of leavening the masses. He exposes the impotency of even Socratic philosophy: he shows, in contrast, the force that works in the words of Jesus; he points out their regenerating power. It is the mission of Justin to be a star in the West, leading its Wise Men to the cradle of Bethlehem.

The writings of Justin are deficient in charms of style; and, for us, there is something the reverse of attractive in the forms of thought which he had learned from the philosophers.[2] If Plato had left us nothing but the Timæus, a Renan would doubtless have reproached him as of feeble intellectual power. So a dancing-master might criticize the movements of an athlete, or the writhings of St. Sebastian shot with arrows. The practical wisdom of Justin using the rhetoric of his times, and discomfiting false philosophy with its own weapons, is not appreciated by the fastidious Parisian. But the manly and heroic pleadings of the man, for a despised people with whom he had boldly identified himself; the intrepidity with which he defends them before despots, whose mere caprice might

---

[1] See Amyot's translation, and a more modern one by De Maistre (*Œuvres*, vol. ii. Paris, 1833). An edition of *The Delays* (the original, with notes by Professor Hackett) has appeared in America (Andover, *circ.*, 1842), and is praised by Tayler Lewis.

[2] He quotes Plato's reference, e.g., to the X.; but the Orientals delighted in such conceits. Compare the Hebrew critics on the ה (in Gen. i. 4), on which see Nordheimer, *Grant.*, vol. i. p.7, New York, 1838.

punish him with death; above all, the undaunted spirit with which he exposes the shame and absurdity of their inveterate superstition and reproaches the memory of Hadrian whom Antoninus had deified, as he had deified Antinous of loathsome history,—these are characteristics which every instinct of the unvitiated soul delights to honour. Justin cannot be refuted by a sneer.

He wore his philosopher's gown after his conversion, as a token that he had attained the only true philosophy. And seeing, that, after the conflicts and tests of ages, it is the only philosophy that lasts and lives and triumphs, its discoverer deserves the homage of mankind. Of the philosophic gown we shall hear again when we come to Tertullian.[3]

The residue of Justin's history may be found in "The Martyrdom" and other pages soon to follow, as well as in the following INTRODUCTORY NOTE of the able translators, Messrs. Dods and Reith:—

JUSTIN MARTYR was born in Flavia Neapolis, a city of Samaria, the modern Nablous. The date of his birth is uncertain, but may be fixed about A.D. 114. His father and grandfather were probably of Roman origin. Before his conversion to Christianity he studied in the schools of the philosophers, searching after some knowledge which should satisfy the cravings of his soul. At last he became acquainted with Christianity, being at once impressed with the extraordinary fearlessness which the Christians displayed in the presence of death, and with the grandeur, stability, and truth of the teachings of the Old Testament. From this time he acted as an evangelist, taking every opportunity to proclaim the gospel as the only safe and certain philosophy, the only way to salvation. It is probable that he travelled much. We know that he was some time in Ephesus, and he must have

---

[3]It survives in the pulpits of Christendom—Greek, Latin, Anglican, Lutheran, etc.—to this day, in slightly different forms.

lived for a considerable period in Rome. Probably he settled in Rome as a Christian teacher. While he was there, the philosophers, especially the Cynics, plotted against him, and he sealed his testimony to the truth by martyrdom.

The principal facts of Justin's life are gathered from his own writings. There is little clue to dates. It is agreed on all hands that he lived in the reign of Antoninus Pius, and the testimony of Eusebius and most credible historians renders it nearly certain that he suffered martyrdom in the reign of Marcus Aurelius. The *Chronicon Paschale* gives as the date 165 A.D.

The writings of Justin Martyr are among the most important that have come down to us from the second century. He was not the first that wrote an Apology in behalf of the Christians, but his Apologies are the earliest extant. They are characterized by intense Christian fervour, and they give us an insight into the relations existing between heathens and Christians in those days. His other principal writing, the Dialogue with Trypho, is the first elaborate exposition of the reasons for regarding Christ as the Messiah of the Old Testament, and the first systematic attempt to exhibit the false position of the Jews in regard to Christianity.

Many of Justin's writings have perished. Those works which have come to us bearing his name have been divided into three classes.

The first class embraces those which are unquestionably genuine, viz. the two Apologies, and Dialogue with Trypho. Some critics have urged objections against Justin's authorship of the Dialogue; but the objections are regarded now as possessing no weight.

The second class consists of those works which are regarded by some critics as Justin's, and by others as not his. They are: 1. An Address to the Greeks; 2. A Hortatory Address to the Greeks; 3. On the Sole Government of God; 4.

An Epistle to Diognetus; 5. Fragments from a work on the Resurrection; 6. And other fragments. Whatever the difficulty there may be in settling the authorship of these treatises, there is but one opinion as to their earliness. The latest of them, in all probability, was not written later than the third century.

The third class consists of those that are unquestionably not the works of Justin. These are: 1. An Exposition of the True Faith; 2. Replies to the Orthodox; 3. Christian Questions to Gentiles; 4. Gentile Questions to Christians; 5. Epistle to Zenas and Serenus; and 6. A Refutation of certain Doctrines of Aristotle. There is no clue to the date of the two last. There can be no doubt that the others were written after the Council of Nicæa, though, immediately after the Reformation, Calvin and others appealed to the first as a genuine writing of Justin's.

There is a curious question connected with the Apologies of Justin which have come down to us. Eusebius mentions two Apologies, —one written in the reign of Antoninus Pius, the other in the reign of Marcus Aurelius. Critics have disputed much whether we have there two Apologies in those now extant. Some have maintained, that what is now called the Second Apology was the preface of the first, and that the second is lost. Others have tried to show that the so-called Second Apology is the continuation of the first, and that the second is lost. Others have supposed that the two Apologies which we have are Justin's two Apologies, but that Eusebius was wrong in affirming that the second was addressed to Marcus Aurelius; and others maintain, that we have in our two Apologies the two Apologies mentioned by Eusebius, and that our first is his first, and our second his second.

THE FIRST APOLOGY OF JUSTIN.

CHAP. I.—ADDRESS.

To the Emperor Titus Ælius Adrianus Antoninus Pius Augustus Cæsar, and to his son Verissimus the Philosopher, and to Lucius the Philosopher, the natural son of Cæsar, and the adopted son of Pius, a lover of learning, and to the sacred Senate, with the whole People of the Romans, I, Justin, the son of Priscus and grandson of Bacchius, natives of Flavia Neapolis in Palestine, present this address and petition in behalf of those of all nations who are unjustly hated and wantonly abused, myself being one of them.

CHAP. II.—JUSTICE DEMANDED.

Reason directs those who are truly pious and philosophical to honour and love only what is true, declining to follow traditional opinions[4], if these be worthless. For not only does sound reason direct us to refuse the guidance of those who did or taught anything wrong, but it is incumbent on the lover of truth, by all means, and if death be threatened, even before his own life, to choose to do and say what is right. Do you, then, since ye are called pious and philosophers, guardians of justice and lovers of learning, give good heed, and hearken to my address; and if ye are indeed such, it will be manifested. For we have come, not to flatter you by this writing, nor please you by our address, but to beg that you pass judgment, after an accurate and searching investigation, not flattered by prejudice or by a desire of pleasing superstitious men, nor induced by irrational impulse or evil rumours which have long been prevalent, to give a decision which will prove to be against

---

[4] Literally, "the opinions of the ancients."

1

yourselves. For as for us, we reckon that no evil can be done us, unless we be convicted as evil-doers, or be proved to be wicked men; and you, you can kill, but not hurt us.

CHAP.III.—CLAIM OF JUDICIAL INVESTIGATION.

But lest any one think that this is an unreasonable and reckless utterance, we demand that the charges against the Christians be investigated, and that, if these be substantiated, they be punished as they deserve; [or rather, indeed, we ourselves will punish them.][5] But if no one can convict us of anything, true reason forbids you, for the sake of a wicked rumour, to wrong blameless men, and indeed rather yourselves, who think fit to direct affairs, not by judgment, but by passion. And every sober-minded person will declare this to be the only fair and equitable adjustment, namely, that the subjects render an unexceptional account of their own life and doctrine; and that, on the other hand, the rulers should give their decision in the obedience, not to violence and tyranny, but to piety, and philosophy. For thus would both rulers and ruled reap benefit. For even one of the ancients somewhere said, "Unless both rulers and ruled philosophize, it is impossible to make states blessed."[6] It is our task, therefore, to afford to all an opportunity of inspecting our life and teachings, lest, on account of those who are accustomed to be ignorant of our affairs, we should incur the penalty due to them for mental blindness;[7] and it is your business, when you hear us, to be found, as reason

---

[5] Thirlby regarded the clause in brackets as an interpolation. There is considerable variety of opinion as to the exact meaning of the words amongst those who regard them as genuine.

[6] Plat. *R. p.*, v. 18.

[7] That is to say, if the Christians refused or neglected to make their real opinions and practices known, they would share the guilt of those whom they thus kept in darkness.

demands, good judges. For if, when ye have learned the truth, you do not what is just, you will be before God without excuse.

CHAP. IV.—CHRISTIANS UNJUSTLY CONDEMNED FOR THEIR MERE NAME.

By the mere application of a name, nothing is decided, either good or evil, apart from the actions implied in the name; and indeed, so far at least as one may judge from the name we are accused of, we are most excellent people.[8] But as we do not think it just to beg to be acquitted on account of the name, if we be convicted as evil-doers, so, on the other hand, if we be found to have committed no offence, either in the matter of thus naming ourselves, or of our conduct as citizens, it is your part very earnestly to guard against incurring just punishment, by unjustly punishing those who are not convicted. For from a name neither praise nor punishment could reasonably spring, unless something excellent or base in action be proved. And those among yourselves who are accused you do not punish before they are convicted; but in our case you receive the name as proof against us, and this although, so far as the name goes, you ought rather to punish our accusers. For we are accused of being Christians, and to hate what is *excellent* (Christian) is unjust. Again, if any of the accused deny the name, and say that he is not a Christian, you acquit him, as having no evidence against him as a wrong-doer; but if any one

---

[8] Justin avails himself here of the similarity in sound of the words Χριστός (Christ) and χρηστός (good, worthy, excellent). The play upon these words is kept up throughout this paragraph, and cannot be always represented to the English reader. [But Justin was merely quoting and using, *ad hominem*, the popular blunder of which Suetonius (*Life of Claudius*, cap. 25) gives us an example, "impulsore *Christo*." It will be observed again in others of these Fathers.]

acknowledge that he is a Christian, you punish him on account of this acknowledgment. Justice requires that you inquire into the life both of him who confesses and of him who denies, that by his deeds it may be apparent what kind of man each is. For as some who have been taught by the Master, Christ, not to deny Him, give encouragement to others when they are put to the question , so in all probability do those who lead wicked lives give occasion to those who, without consideration, take upon them to accuse all the Christians of impiety and wickedness. And this also is not right. For of philosophy, too, some assume the name and the garb who do nothing worthy of their profession; and you are aware, that those of the ancients whose opinions and teachings were quite diverse, are yet all called by the one name of philosophers. And of these some taught atheism; and the poets who have flourished among you raise a laugh out of the uncleanness of Jupiter with his own children. And those who now adopt such instruction are not restrained by you; but, on the contrary, you bestow prizes and honours upon those who euphoniously insult the gods.

CHAP. V.—CHRISTIANS CHARGED WITH ATHEISM.

Why, then, should this be? In our case, who pledge ourselves to do no wickedness, nor to hold these atheistic opinions, you do not examine the charges made against us; but, yielding to unreasoning passion, and to the instigation of evil demons, you punish us without consideration or judgment. For the truth shall be spoken; since of old these evil demons, effecting apparitions of themselves, both defiled women and corrupted boys, and showed such fearful sights to men, that those who did not use their reason in judging of the actions that were done, were struck with terror; and being carried away by fear, and not knowing that these were demons, they called them gods, and gave to each the name which each of the demons chose for himself.[9] And when Socrates endeavoured, by true reason and examination, to bring these things to light, and deliver men from the demons, then the demons themselves, by means of men who rejoiced in iniquity, compassed his death, as an atheist and a profane person, on the charge that "he was introducing new divinities;" and in our case they display a similar activity. For not only among the Greeks did reason (Logos) prevail to condemn these things through Socrates, but also among the Barbarians were they condemned by Reason (or the Word, the Logos) Himself, who took shape, and became man, and was called Jesus Christ; and in obedience to Him, we not only deny that they who did such things as these are gods,[10] but assert that they are wicked and impious demons, whose actions will not bear comparison with those even of men desirous of virtue.

CHAP. VI.—CHARGE OF ATHEISM REFUTED.

Hence are we called atheists. And we confess that we are atheists, so far as gods of this sort are concerned, but not with respect to the most true God, the Father of righteousness and temperance and the other virtues, who is free from all impurity. But both Him, and the Son (who came forth from Him and taught us these things, and the host of

---

[9] [I. Cor. X. 20, Milton's admirable economy in working this truth into his great poem (i. 378) affords a sublime exposition of the mind of the Fathers on the origin of mythologies.]

[10] The word δαίμων means in Greek a god, but the Christians used the word to signify an evil spirit. Justin uses the same word here for god and demon. The connection which Justin and other Christian writers supposed to exist between evil spirits and the gods of the heathens will be apparent from Justin's own statements. The word διάβολος, devil, is not applied to these demons. There is but one devil, but many demons.

the other good angels who follow and are made like to Him),[11] and the prophetic Spirit, we worship and adore, knowing them in reason and truth, and declaring without grudging to every one who wishes to learn, as we have been taught.

CHAP. VII.—EACH CHRISTIAN MUST BE TRIED BY HIS OWN LIFE.

But some one will say, Some have ere now been arrested and convicted as evil-doers. For you condemn many, many a time, after inquiring into the life of each of the accused severally, but not on account of those of whom we have been speaking.[12] And this we acknowledge, that as among the Greeks those who teach such theories as please themselves are called by the one name "Philosopher," though their doctrines be diverse, so also among the Barbarians this name on which accusations are accumulated is the common property of those who are and those who seem wise. For all are called Christians. Wherefore we demand that the deeds of all those who are accused to you be judged, in order that

---

[11]This is the literal and obvious translation of Justin's words. But from c. 13, 16, and 61, it is evident that he did not desire to inculcate the worship of angels. We are therefore driven to adopt another translation of this passage, even though it be somewhat harsh. Two such translations have been proposed: the first connecting "us" and "the host of the other good angels" as the common object of the verb "taught:" the second connecting "these things" with "the host of," etc., and making these two together the subject taught. In the first case the translation would stand, "taught these things to us and to the host," etc.: in the second case the translation would be, "taught us about these things, and about the host of the others who follow Him, viz. the good angels." [I have ventured to insert parenthetic marks in the text, an obvious and simple resource to suggest the manifest intent of the author. Grabe's note *in loc.* gives another and very ingenious exegesis, but the simplest is best.]

[12] i.e., according to Otto, "not on account of the sincere Christians of whom we have been speaking." According to Trollope, "not on account of (or at the instigation of) the demons before mentioned."

each one who is convicted may be punished as an evil-doer, and not as a Christian; and if it is clear that any one is blameless, that he may be acquitted, since by the mere fact of his being a Christian he does no wrong.[13] For we will not require that you punish our accusers;[14] they being sufficiently punished by their present wickedness and ignorance of what is right.

CHAP. VIII.—CHRISTIANS CONFESS THEIR FAITH IN GOD.

And reckon ye that it is for your sakes we have been saying these things; for it is in our power, when we are examined, to deny that we are Christians; but we would not live by telling a lie. For, impelled by the desire of the eternal and pure life, we seek the abode that is with God, the Father and Creator of all, and hasten to confess our faith, persuaded and convinced as we are that they who have proved to God[15] by their works that they followed Him, and loved to abide with Him where there is no sin to cause disturbance, can obtain these things. This, then, to speak shortly, is what we expect and have learned from Christ, and teach. And Plato, in like manner, used to say that Rhadamanthus and Minos would punish the wicked who came before them; and we say that the same thing will be done, but at the hand of Christ, and upon the wicked in the same bodies united again to their spirits which are now to undergo everlasting punishment; and not only, as Plato said, for a period of a thousand years. And if any one say that this is incredible or impossible, this error of ours is one which concerns ourselves only, and no

---

[13] Or, "as a Christian who has done no wrong."
[14] Compare the Rescript of Adrian appended to this Apology.
[15] Literally, "persuaded God."

other person, so long as you cannot convict us of doing any harm.

CHAP. IX.—FOLLY OF IDOL WORSHIP.

And neither do we honour with many sacrifices and garlands of flowers such deities as men have formed and set in shrines and called gods; since we see that these are soulless and dead, and have not the form of God (for we do not consider that God has such a form as some say that they imitate to His honour), but have the names and forms of those wicked demons which have appeared. For why need we tell you who already know, into what forms the craftsmen,[16] carving and cutting, casting and hammering, fashion the materials? And often out of vessels of dishonour, by merely changing the form, and making an image of the requisite shape, they make what they call a god; which we consider not only senseless, but to be even insulting to God, who, having ineffable glory and form, thus gets His name attached to things that are corruptible, and require constant service. And that the artificers of these are both intemperate, and, not to enter into particulars, are practiced in every vice, you very well know; even their own girls who work along with them they corrupt. What infatuation! That dissolute men should be said to fashion and make gods for your worship, and that you should appoint such men the guardians of the temples where they are enshrined; not recognising that it is unlawful even to think or say that men are the guardians of gods.

---

[16] [Isa. Xliv. 9-30; Jer. X. 3.]

CHAP. X.—HOW GOD IS TO BE SERVED.

But we have received by tradition that God does not need the material offerings which men can give, seeing, indeed, that He Himself is the provider of all things. And we have been taught, and are convinced, and do believe, that He accepts those only who imitate the excellences which reside in Him, temperance, and justice, and philanthropy, and as many virtues as are peculiar to a God who is called by no proper name. And we have been taught that He in the beginning did of His goodness, for man's sake, create all things out of unformed matter; and if men by their works show themselves worthy of this His design, they are deemed worthy, and so we have received—of reigning in company with Him, being delivered from corruption and suffering. For as in the beginning He created us when we were not, so do we consider that, in like manner, those who choose what is pleasing to Him are, on account of their choice, deemed worthy of incorruption and of fellowship with Him. For the coming into being at first was not in our own power; and in order that we may follow those things which please Him, choosing them by means of the rational faculties He has Himself endowed us with, He both persuades us and leads us to faith. And we think it for the advantage of all men that they are not restrained from learning these things, but are even urged thereto. For the restraint which human laws could not effect, the Word, inasmuch as He is divine, would have effected, had not the wicked demons, taking as their ally the lust of wickedness which is in every man, and which draws variously to all manner of vice, scattered many false and profane accusations, none of which attach to us.

CHAP. XI.—WHAT KINGDOM CHRISTIANS LOOK FOR.

And when you hear that we look for a kingdom, you suppose, without making any inquiry, that we speak of a human kingdom; whereas we speak of that which is with God, as appears also from the confession of their faith made by those who are charged with being Christians, though they know that death is the punishment awarded to him who so confesses. For if we looked for a human kingdom, we should also deny our Christ, that we might not be slain; and we should strive to escape detection, that we might obtain what we expect. But since our thought are not fixed on the present, we are not concerned when men cut us off; since also death is a debt which must at all events be paid.

CHAP. XII.—CHRISTIANS LIVE AS UNDER GOD'S EYE.

And more than all other men are we your helpers and allies in promoting peace, seeing that we hold this view, that it is alike impossible for the wicked, the covetous, the conspirator, and for the virtuous, to escape the notice of God, and that each man goes to everlasting punishment or salvation according to the value of his actions. For if all men knew this, no one would choose wickedness even for a little, knowing that he goes to the everlasting punishment of fire; but would by all means restrain himself, and adorn himself with virtue, that he might obtain the good gifts of God, and escape the punishments. For those who, on account of the laws and punishments you impose, endeavour to escape detection when they offend (and they offend, too, under the impression that it is quite possible to escape your detection, since you are but men), those persons, if they learned and were convinced that nothing whether actually done or only intended, can escape the knowledge of God, would be all means live decently on account of the penalties threatened, as even you yourselves will admit. But you seem to fear lest all men become righteous, and you no longer have any to punish. Such would be the concern of public executioners, but not of good princes. But, as we before said, we are persuaded that these things are prompted by evil spirits, who demand sacrifices and service even from those who live unreasonably; but as for you, we presume that you who aim at [a reputation for] piety and philosophy will do nothing unreasonable. But if you also, like the foolish, prefer custom to truth, do what you have the power to do. But just so much power have rulers who esteem opinion more than truth, as robbers have in a desert. And that you will not succeed is declared by the Word, than whom, after God who begat Him, we know there is no ruler more kingly and just. For as all shrink from succeeding to the poverty or sufferings or obscurity of their fathers, so whatever the Word forbids us to choose, the sensible man will not choose. That all these things should come to pass, I say, our Teacher foretold, He who is both Son and Apostle of God the Father of all and the Ruler, Jesus Christ; from whom also we have the name of Christians. Whence we become more assured of all the things He taught us, since whatever He beforehand foretold should come to pass, is seen in fact coming to pass; and this is the work of God, to tell of a thing before it happens, and as it was foretold so to show it happening. It were possible to pause here and add no more, reckoning that we demand what is just and true; but because we are well aware that it is not easy suddenly to change a mind possessed by ignorance, we intend to add a few things, for the sake of persuading those who love the truth, knowing that it is not impossible to put ignorance to flight by presenting the truth.

CHAP. XIII.—CHRISTIANS SERVE GOD RATIONALLY

What sober-minded man, then will not acknowledge that we are not atheists, worshipping as we do the Maker of this universe, and declaring, as we have been taught, that He has no need of streams of blood and libations and incense; whom we praise to the utmost of our power by the exercise of prayer and thanksgiving for all things wherewith we are supplied, as we have been taught that the only honour that is worthy of Him is not to consume by fire what He has brought into being for our sustenance, but to use it for ourselves and those who need, and with gratitude to Him to offer thanks by invocations and hymns[17] for our creation, and for all the means of health, and for the various qualities of the different kinds of things, and for the changes of the seasons; and to present before Him petitions for our existing again in incorruption through faith in Him. Our teacher of these things is Jesus Christ, who also was born for this purpose, and was crucified under Pontius Pilate, procurator of Judæa, in the times of Tiberius Cæsar; and that we reasonably worship Him, having learned that He is the Son of the true God Himself, and holding Him in the second place, and the prophetic Spirit in the third, we will prove. For they proclaim our madness to consist in this, that we give to a crucified man a place second to the unchangeable and eternal God, the Creator of all; for they do not discern the mystery that is herein, to which, as we make it plain to you, we pray you to give heed.

---

[17] πομπάς καί ὕμνους."Grabe, and it should seem correctly, understands πομπάς to be *solemn prayers*... He also remarks, that the ὕμνοι were either psalms of David, or some of those psalms and songs made by the primitive Christians, which are mentioned in Eusebius, *H. E.*, v. 28."— Trollope.

CHAP. XIV.—THE DEMONS MISREPRESENT CHRISTIAN DOCTRINE.

For we forewarn you to be on your guard, lest those demons whom we have been accusing should deceive you, and quite divert you from reading and understanding what we say. For they strive to hold you their slaves and servants; and sometimes by appearances in dreams, and sometimes by magical impositions, they subdue all who make no strong opposing effort for their own salvation. And thus do we also, since our persuasion by the Word, stand aloof from them (i.e., the demons), and follow the only unbegotten God through His Son—we who formerly delighted in fornication, but now embrace chastity alone; we who formerly used magical arts, dedicate ourselves to the good and unbegotten God; we who valued above all things the acquisition of wealth and possessions, now bring what we have into a common stock, and communicate to every one in need; we who hated and destroyed one another, and on account of their different manners would not live[18] with men of a different tribe, now, since the coming of Christ, live familiarly with them, and pray for our enemies, and endeavour to persuade those who hate use unjustly to live comfortable to the good precepts of Christ, to the end that they may become partakers with us of the same joyful hope of a reward from God the ruler of all. But lest we should seem to be reasoning sophistically, we consider it right, before giving you the promised[19] explanation, to cite a few precepts given by Christ Himself. And be it yours, as powerful rulers, to inquire whether we have been taught and do teach these things truly. Brief and concise utterances fell

---

[18] Literally, "would not use the same hearth or fire."
[19] See the end of chap. Xii.

13

from Him, for He was no sophist, but His word was the power of God.

CHAP. XV.—WHAT CHRIST HIMSELF TAUGHT

Concerning chastity, He uttered such sentiments as these:[20] "Whosoever looketh upon a woman to lust after her, hath committed adultery with her already in his heart before God." And, "If thy right eye offend thee, cut it out; for it is better for thee to enter into the kingdom of heaven with one eye, than, having two eyes, to be cast into everlasting fire." And, "Whosoever shall marry her that is divorced from another husband, committeth adultery."[21] And, "There are some who have been made eunuchs of men, and some who were born eunuchs, and some who have made themselves eunuchs for the kingdom of heaven's sake; but all cannot receive this saying."[22] So that all who, by human law, are twice married,[23] are in the eye of our Master sinners, and those who look upon a woman to lust after her. For not only he who in act commits adultery is rejected by Him, but also he who desires to commit adultery: since not only our works, but also our thoughts, are open before God. And many, both men and women, who have been Christ's disciples from childhood, remain pure at the age of sixty or seventy years; and I boast that I could produce such from every race of

---

[20] The reader will notice that Justin quotes from memory, so that there are some slight discrepancies between the words of Jesus as here cited, and the same sayings as recorded in our Gospels.

[21] Matt. V. 28, 29, 32.

[22] Matt. Xix. 12.

[23] , lit. contracting a double marriage. Of double marriages there are three kind: the first, marriage with a second wife while the first is still alive and recognized as a lawful wife, or bigamy; the second, marriage with a second wife after divorce from the first; and third, marriage with a second wife after the death of the first. It is thought that Justin here refers to the second case.

men. For what shall I say, too, of the countless multitude of those who have reformed intemperate habits, and learned these things? For Christ called not the just nor the chaste to repentance, but the ungodly, and the licentious, and the unjust; His word being, "I came not to call the righteous, but sinners to repentance."[24] For the heavenly Father desires rather the repentance than the punishment of the sinner. And of our love to all, He taught thus: "If ye love them that love you, what new thing do ye? For even fornicators do this. But I say unto you, Pray for your enemies, and love them that hate you, and bless them that curse you, and pray for them that despitefully use you."[25] And that we should communicate to the needy, and do nothing for glory, He said, "Give to him that asketh, and from him that would borrow turn not away; for if ye lend to them of whom ye hope to receive, what new thing do ye? Even the publicans do this. Lay not up for yourselves treasure upon earth, where moth and rust doth corrupt, and where robbers break through; but lay up for yourselves treasure in heaven, where neither moth nor rust doth corrupt. For what is a man profited, if he shall gain the whole world, and lose his own soul? Or what shall a man give in exchange for it? Lay up treasure, therefore, in heaven, where neither moth nor rust doth corrupt."[26] And, "Be ye kind and merciful, as your Father also is kind and merciful, and maketh His sun to rise on sinners, and the righteous, and the wicked. Take no thought what ye shall eat, or what ye shall put on: are ye not better than the birds and the beasts? And God feedeth them. Take no thought, therefore, what ye shall eat, or what ye shall put on; for your heavenly Father knoweth that ye have need of these things. But seek ye the kingdom of heaven, and all these things shall

---

[24] Matt. Ix. 13.
[25] Matt. V. 46, 44; Luke vi. 28.
[26]Luke vi. 30, 34; Matt. Vi. 19, xvi. 26, vi. 20.

be added unto you. For where his treasure is, there also is the mind of a man."[27] And, "Do not these things to be seen of men; otherwise ye have no reward from your Father which is in heaven."[28]

CHAP. XVI.—CONCERNING PATIENCE AND SWEARING.

And concerning our being patient of injuries, and ready to serve all, and free from anger, this is what He said: "To him that smiteth thee on the one cheek, offer also the other; and him that taketh away they cloak, forbid not. And whosoever shall be angry, is in danger of the fire. And every one that compelleth thee to go with him a mile, follow him two. And let your good works shine before men, that they, seeing them, may glorify your Father which is in heaven."[29] For we ought not to strive; neither has He desired us to be imitators of wicked men, but He has exhorted us to lead all men, by patience and gentleness, from shame and the love of evil. And this indeed is proved in the case of many who once were of your way of thinking, but have changed their violent and tyrannical disposition, being overcome either by the constancy which they have witnessed in their neighbour's lives,[30] or by the extraordinary forbearance they have observed in their fellow-travellers when defrauded, or by the honesty of those with whom they have transacted business.

And with regard to our not swearing at all, and always speaking the truth, He enjoined as follows: "Swear not at all; but let your yea be yea, and your nay, nay; for whatsoever is more than these cometh of evil."[31] And that we ought to

---

[27] Luke vi. 36; Matt. v. 45, vi. 25, 26, 33, 21.
[28] Matt. vi. 1.
[29] Luke vi. 29; Matt. vi. 22, 41, 16.
[30] i.e., Christian neighbours.
[31] Matt. v. 34, 27.

worship God alone, He thus persuaded us: "The greatest commandment is, Thou shalt worship the Lord thy God, and Him only shalt thou serve, with all thy heart, and with all thy strength, the Lord God that made thee."[32] And when a certain man came to Him and said, "Good Master," He answered and said, "There is none good but God only, who made all things."[33] And let those who are not found living as He taught, be understood to be no Christians, even though they profess with the lip of precepts of Christ; for not those who make profession, but those who do the works, shall be saved, according to His word: "Not every one who saith to Me, Lord, Lord, shall enter into the kingdom of heaven, but he that doeth the will of My Father which is in heaven. For whosoever heareth Me, and doeth My sayings, heareth Him that sent Me. And many will say unto Me, Lord, Lord, have we not eaten and drunk in Thy name, and done wonders? And then will I say unto them, Depart from Me, ye workers of iniquity. Then shall there be wailing and gnashing of teeth, when the righteous shall shine as the sun, and the wicked are sent into everlasting fire. For many shall come in My name, clothed outwardly in sheep's clothing, but inwardly being ravening wolves. By their works ye shall know them. And every tree that bringeth not forth good fruit, is hewn down and cast into the fire."[34] And as to those who are not living pursuant to these His teachings, and are Christians only in name, we demand that all such be punished by you.

---

[32] Mark xii. 30.
[33] Matt. xix. 6, 17.
[34] Matt. vii. 21, etc.; Luke xiii. 26; Matt. xiii. 42, vii. 15, 16, 19.

CHAP. XVII.—CHRIST
TAUGHT CIVIL OBEDIENCE.

And everywhere we, more readily than all men, endeavour to pay to those appointed by you the taxes both ordinary and extraordinary,[35] as we have been taught by Him; for at that time some came to Him and asked Him, if one ought to pay tribute to Cæsar; and He answered, "Tell Me, whose image does the coin bear?" And they said, "Cæsar's." And again He answered them, "Render therefore to Cæsar the things that are Cæsar's, and to God the things that are God's."[36] Whence to God alone we render worship, but in other things we gladly serve you, acknowledging you as kings and rulers of men, and praying that with your kingly power you be found to possess also sound judgment. But if you pay no regard to our prayers and frank explanations, we shall suffer no loss since we believe (or rather, indeed, are persuaded) that every man will suffer punishment in eternal fire according to the merit of his deed, and will render account according to the power he has received from God, as Christ intimated when He said, "To whom God has given more, of him shall more be required."[37]

CHAP. XVIII.—PROOF OF
IMMORTALITY AND THE RESURRECTION.

For reflect upon the end of each of the preceding kings, how they died the death common to all, which, if it issued in insensibility, would be a godsend[38] to all the wicked. But

---

[35] Φόρους καί εἰσφοράςThe former is the annual tribute; the latter, any occasional assessment. See Otto's Note, and Thucyd. Iii. 19.

[36] Matt. xxii. 17, 19, 20, 21.

[37] Luke xii. 48.

[38] ἕρμαιον, a piece of unlooked-for luck, Hermes being the reputed giver of such gifts: vid. Liddell and Scott's Lex.; see also scholiast, quoted by

since sensation remains to all who have ever lived, and eternal punishment is laid up (i.e., for the wicked), see that ye neglect not to be convinced, and to hold as your belief, that these things are true. For let even necromancy, and the divinations you practice by immaculate children,[39] and the evoking of departed human souls,[40] and those who are called among the magi, Dream-senders and Assistant-spirits (Familiars),[41] and all that is done by those who are skilled in such matters—let these persuade you that even after death souls are in a state of sensation; and those who are seized and cast about by the spirits of the dead, whom all call dæmoniacs or madmen;[42] and what you repute as oracles, both of Amphilochus, Dodana, Pytho, and as many other such as exist; and the opinions of your authors, Empedocles and Pythagoras, Plato and Socrates, and the pit of Homer,[43]

Stallbaum in Plato's *Phaed.*, p. 107, on a passage singularly analogous to this.

[39] Boys and girls, or even children prematurely taken from the womb, were slaughtered, and their entrail inspected, in the belief that the souls of the victims (being still conscious, as Justin is arguing) would reveal things hidden and future. Instances are abundantly cited by Otto and Trollope.

[40] This form of spirit-rapping was familiar to the ancients, and Justin again (*Dial. C. Tryph.*, c. 105) uses the invocation of Samuel by the witch of Endor as a proof of the immortality of the soul.

[41] Valesius (on Euseb. *H. E.*, iv. 7) states that the magi had two kinds of familiars: the first, who were sent to inspire men with dreams which might give them intimations of things future; and the second, who were sent to watch over men, and protect them from diseases and misfortunes. The first, he says, they called (as here), ὀνειροπομπούς and the second παρέδους.

[42] Justin is not the only author in ancient or recent times who has classed dæmoniacs and maniacs together; neither does he stand alone among the ancients in the opinion that dæmoniacs were possessed by the spirits of departed men. References will be found in Trollope's note. [See this matter more fully illustrated in Kaye's *Justin Martyr*, pp. 105-111.]

[43] See the *Odyssey*, book xi. Line 25, where Ulysses is described as digging a pit or trench with his sword, and pouring libations, in order to collect around him the souls of the dead.

and the descent of Ulysses to inspect these things, and all that has been uttered of a like kind. Such favour as you grant to these, grant also to us, who not less but more firmly than they believe in God; since we expect to receive again our own bodies, though they be dead and cast into the earth, for we maintain that with God nothing is impossible.

CHAP. XIX.—THE RESURRECTION POSSIBLE.

And to any thoughtful person would anything appear more incredible, than, if we were not in the body, and some one were to say that it was possible that from a small drop of human seed bones and sinews and flesh be formed into a shape such as we see? For let this now be said hypothetically: if you yourselves were not such as you now are, and born of such parent [and causes], and one were to show you human seed and a picture of a man and were to say with confidence that from such a substance such a being could be produced, would you believe before you saw the actual production? No one will dare to deny [that such a statement would surpass belief]. In the same way, then, you are now incredulous because you have never seen a dead man rise again. But as at first you would not have believed it possible that such persons could be produced from the small drop, and yet now you see them thus produced, so also judge ye that it is not impossible that the bodies of men, after they have been dissolved, and like seeds resolved into the earth, should in God's appointed time rise again and put on incorruption. For what power worthy of God those imagine who say, that each thing returns to that from which it was produced, and that beyond this not even God Himself can do anything, we are unable to conceive; but this we see clearly, that they would not have believed it possible that they could have become such and produced from such materials, as they now see both themselves and the whole world to be. And that it is better to believe even what is impossible to our own nature and to men, than to be unbelieving like the rest of the world, we have learned; for we know that our Master Jesus Christ said, that "what is impossible with men is possible with God,"[44] and, "Fear not them that kill you, and after that can do no more; but fear Him who after death is able to cast both soul and body into hell."[45] And hell is a place where those are to be punished who have lived wickedly, and who do not believe that those things which God has taught us by Christ will come to pass.

CHAP. XX.—HEATHEN ANALOGIES TO CHRISTIAN DOCTRINE.

And the Sibyl[46] and Hystaspes said that there should be a dissolution by God of things corruptible. And the philosophers called Stoics teach that even God Himself shall be resolved into fire, and they say that the world is to be formed anew by this revolution; but we understand that God, the Creator of all things, is superior to the things that are to be changed. If, therefore, on some points we teach the same things as the poets and philosophers whom you honour, and on other points are fuller and more divine in our teaching, and if we alone afford proof of what we assert, why are we

---

[44] Matt. xix. 26.

[45] Matt. x. 28.

[46] The Sibylline Oracles are now generally regarded as heathen fragments largely interpolated by unscrupulous men during the early ages of the Church. For an interesting account of these somewhat perplexing documents, see Burton's *Lectures on the Ecclesiastical History of the First Three Centuries*, Lect. xvii. The prophecies of Hystaspes were also commonly appealed to as genuine by the early Christians. [See (on the Sibyls and Justin M.) Casaubon, *Exercitationes*, pp. 65 and 80. This work is a most learned and diversified *thesaurus*, in the form of strictures on Card. Baronius. Geneva, 1663.]

unjustly hated more than all others? For while we say that all things have been produced and arranged into a world by God, we shall seem to utter the doctrine of Plato; and while we say that there will be a burning up of all, we shall seem to utter the doctrine of the Stoics: and while we affirm that the souls of the wicked, being endowed with sensation even after death, are punished, and that those of the good being delivered from punishment spend a blessed existence, we shall seem to say the same things as the poets and philosophers; and while we maintain that men ought not to worship the works of their hands we say the very things which have been said by the comic poet Menander, and other similar writers, for they have declared that the workman is greater than the work.

CHAP. XXI.—ANALOGIES
TO THE HISTORY OF CHRIST.

And when we say also that the Word, who is the first-birth[47] of God, was produced without sexual union, and that He, Jesus Christ, our Teacher, was crucified and died, and rose again, and ascended into heaven, we propound nothing different from what you believe regarding those whom you esteem sons of Jupiter. For you know how many sons your esteemed writers ascribed to Jupiter: Mercury, the interpreting word and teacher of all; Æsculapius, who, though he was a great physician, was struck by a thunderbolt, and so ascended to heaven; and Bacchus too, after he had been torn limb from limb; and Hercules, when he had committed himself to the flames to escape his toils; and the sons of Leda, and Dioscuri; and Perseus, son of Danae; and Bellerophon, who, though sprung from mortals, rose to heaven on the horse Pegasus. For what shall I say of

---

[47] i.e., first-born.

Ariadne, and those who, like her have been declared to be set among the stars? And what of the emperors who die among yourselves, whom you deem worthy of deification, and in whose behalf you produce some one who swears he has seen the burning Cæsar rise to heaven fro the funeral pyre? And what kind of deeds are recorded of each of these reputed sons of Jupiter, it is needless to tell to those who already know. This only shall be said, that they are written for the advantage and encouragement[48] of youthful scholars; for all reckon it an honourable thing to imitate the gods. But far be such a thought concerning the gods from every well-conditioned soul, as to believe that Jupiter himself, the governor and creator of all things, was both a parricide and the son of a parricide, and that being overcome by the love of base and shameful pleasures, he came in to Ganymede and those many women whom he had violated and that his sons did like actions. But, as we said above, wicked devils perpetrated these things. And we have learned that those only are deified who have lived near to God in holiness and virtue; and we believe that those who live wickedly and do not repent are punished in everlasting fire.

CHAP. XXII.—ANALOGIES
TO THE SONSHIP OF CHRIST.

Moreover, the Son of God called Jesus, even if only a man by ordinary generation, yet, on account of His wisdom, is worthy to be called the Son of God; for all writers call God the Father of men and gods. And if we assert that the Word

---

[48] διαφοράν καί προτροπήν. The irony here is so obvious as to make the proposed reading (διαφθοράν καί παρτροπήν, corruption and depravation) unnecessary. Otto prefers the reading adopted above. Trollope, on the other hand, inclines to the latter reading, mainly on the score of the former expressions being unusual. See his very sensible note *in loc.*

of God was born of God in a peculiar manner, different from ordinary generation, let this, as said above, be no extraordinary thing to you, who say that Mercury is the angelic word of God. But if any one objects that He was crucified, in this also He is on a par with those reputed sons of Jupiter of yours, who suffered as we have new enumerated. For their sufferings at death are recorded to have been not all alike, but diverse; so that not even by the peculiarity of His sufferings does He seem to be inferior to them; but, on the contrary, as we promised in the preceding part of this discourse, we will now prove Him superior—or rather have already proved Him to be so—for the superior is revealed by His actions. And if we even affirm that He was born of a virgin, accept this in common with what you accept of Perseus. And in that we say that He made whole the lame, the paralytic, and those born blind, we seem to say what is very similar to the deeds said to have been done by Æsculapius.

CHAP. XXIII.—THE ARGUMENT.

And that this may now become evident to you—(firstly[49]) that whatever we assert in conformity with what has been taught us by Christ, and by the prophets who preceded Him, are alone true, and are older than all the writers who have existed; that we claim to be acknowledged, not because we

---

[49] The Benedictine editor, Maranus, Otto, and Trollope, here note that Justin in this chapter promises to make good three distinct positions: 1st, That Christian doctrines alone are true, and are to be received, not on account of their resemblance to the sentiments of poets or philosophers, but on their own account; 2nd, that Jesus Christ is the incarnate Son of God, and our teacher; 3rd, that before His incarnation, the demons, having some knowledge of what He would accomplish, enabled the heathen poets and priests in some points to anticipate, though in a distorted form, the facts of the incarnation. The first he establishes in chap. xxiv-xxix.; the second in chap xxx.-liii.; and the third in chap. liv. et sq.

say the same things as these writers said, but because we say true things: and (secondly) that Jesus Christ is the only proper Son who has been begotten by God, being His Word and first-begotten, and power; and, becoming man according to His will, He taught us these things for the conversion and restoration of the human race: and (thirdly) that before He became a man among men, some, influenced by the demons before mentioned, related beforehand, through the instrumentality of the poets, those circumstances as having really happened, which, having fictitiously devised, they narrated, in the same manner as they have caused to be fabricated the scandalous reports against us of infamous and impious actions,[50] of which there is neither witness nor proof—we shall bring forward the following proof.

CHAP. XXIV.—VARIETIES OF HEATHEN WORSHIP.

In the first place [we furnish proof], because, though we say things similar to what the Greeks say, we only are hated on account of the name of Christ, and though we do no wrong, are put to death as sinners; other men in other places worshipping trees and rivers, and mice and cats and crocodiles, and many irrational animals. Nor are the same animals esteemed by all; but in one place one is worshipped, and another in another, so that all are profane in the judgment of one another, on account of their not worshipping the same objects. And this is the sole accusation you bring against us, that we do not reverence the same gods as you do, nor offer to the dead libations and the savour of fat, and crowns for their statues,[51] and sacrifices. For you

---

[50] We have here followed the reading and rendering of Trollope. [But see reading of Langus, and Grabe's note, in the edition already cited, 1. 46.]

[51] ἐν γραφαῖς στεφάνους. The only conjecture which seems at all probable is that of the Benedictine editor followed here. [Grabe after

25

very well know that the same animals are with some esteemed gods, with others wild beasts, and with others sacrificial victims.

CHAP. XXV.—FALSE GODS ABANDONED BY CHRISTIANS.

And, secondly, because we—who, out of every race of men, used to worship Bacchus the son of Semele, and Apollo the son of Latona (who in their loves with men did such things as it is shameful even to mention), and Proserpine and Venus (who were maddened with love of Adonis, and whose mysteries also you celebrate), or Æsculapius, or some one or other of those who are called gods—have now, through Jesus Christ, learned to despise these, though we be threatened with death for it, and have dedicated ourselves to the unbegotten and impassible God; of whom we are persuaded that never was he goaded by lust of Antiope, or such other women, or of Ganymede, nor was rescued by that hundred-handed giant whose aid was obtained through Thetis, nor was anxious on this account[52] that her son Achilles should destroy many of the Greeks because of his concubine Briseis. Those who believe these things we pity, and those who invented them we know to be devils.

CHAP. XXVI.—MAGICIANS NOT TRUSTED BY CHRISTIANS.

And, thirdly, because after Christ's ascension into heaven the devils put forward certain men who said that they themselves were gods; and they were not only not persecuted

Salmasius reads εν 'ραφαΐς and quotes Martial, *Sutilis aptetur rosa crinibus*. Translate, "patch-work garlands."]
[52] i.e., on account of the assistance gained for him by Thetis, and in return for it.

by you, but even deemed worthy of honours. There was a Samaritan, Simon, a native of the village called Gitto, who in the reign of Claudius Cæsar, and in your royal city of Rome, did mighty acts of magic, by virtue of the art of the devils operating in him. He was considered a god, and as a god was honoured by you with a statue, which statue was erected on the river Tiber, between the two bridges, and bore this inscription, in the language of Rome:—

"Simoni Deo Sancto,"[53] — "To Simon the holy God."

And almost all the Samaritans, and a few even of other nations, worship him, and acknowledge him as the first god; and a woman, Helena, who went about with him at that time, and had formerly been a prostitute, they say is the first idea generated by him. And a man, Meander, also a Samaritan, of the town Capparetæa, a disciple of Simon, and inspired by devils, we know to have deceived many while he was in Antioch by his magical art. He persuaded those who adhered to him that they should never die, and even now there are some living who hold this opinion of his. And there is Marcion, a man of Pontus, who is even at this day alive, and teaching his disciples to believe in some other god greater than the Creator. And he, by the aid of the devils, has caused

---

[53] It is very generally supposed that Justin was mistaken in understanding this to have been a statue erected to Simon Magus. This supposition rests on the fact that in the year 1574 there was dug up in the island of the Tiber a fragment of marble, with the inscription "Semoni Sanco Deo," etc., being probably the base of a statue erected to the Sabine deity Semo Sancus. This inscription Justin is supposed to have mistaken for the one he gives above. This has always seemed to us very slight evidence on which to reject so precise a statement as Justin here makes; a statement which he would scarcely have hazarded in an apology addressed to Rome, where every person had the means of ascertaining its accuracy. If, as is supposed, he made a mistake, it must have been at once exposed, and other writers would not have so frequently repeated the story as they have done. See *Burton's Bampton Lectures*, p. 374- [See Note in Grabe (1. 51), and also mine, at end.]

many of every nation to speak blasphemies, and to deny that God is the maker of this universe, and to assert that some other being, greater than He, has done greater works. All who take their opinions from these men, are, as we before said,[54] called Christians; just as also those who do not agree with the philosophers in their doctrines, have yet in common with them the name of philosophers given to them. And whether they perpetrate those fabulous and shameful deeds[55]—the upsetting of the lamp, and promiscuous intercourse, and eating human flesh—we know not; but we do know that they are neither persecuted nor put to death by you, at least on account of their opinions. But I have a treatise against all the heresies that have existed already composed, which, if you wish to read it, I will give you.

CHAP. XXVII.—GUILT OF EXPOSING CHILDREN.

But as for us, we have been taught that to expose newly-born children is the part of wicked men; and this we have been taught lest we should do any one an injury, and lest we should sin against God, first, because we see that almost all so exposed (not only the girls, but also the males) are brought up to prostitution. And as the ancients are said to have reared herds of oxen, or goats, or sheep, or grazing horses, so now we see you rear children only for this shameful use; and for this pollution a multitude of females and hermaphrodites, and those who commit unmentionable iniquities, are found in every nation. And you receive the hire of these, and duty and taxes from them, whom you ought to exterminate from your realm. And any one who uses such persons, besides the godless and infamous and impure intercourse, may possibly be having intercourse with

---

[54] See chap. vii.

[55] Which were commonly charged against the Christians.

his own child, or relative, or brother. And there are some who prostitute even their own children and wives, and some are openly mutilated for the purpose of sodomy; and they refer these mysteries to the mother of the gods, and along with each of those whom you esteem gods there is painted a serpent,[56] a great symbol and mystery. Indeed, the things[57] which you do openly and with applause, as if the divine light were overturned and extinguished, these you lay to our charge; which, in truth, does no harm to us who shrink from doing any such things, but only to those who do them and bear false witness against us.

CHAP. XXVIII.—GOD'S CARE FOR MEN.

For among us the prince of the wicked spirits is called the serpent, and Satan, and the devil, as you can learn by looking into our writings. And that he would be sent into the fire with his host, and the men who follow him, and would be punished for an endless duration, Christ foretold. For the reason why God has delayed to do this, is His regard for the human race. For He foreknows that some are to be saved by repentance, some even that are perhaps not yet born.[58] In the beginning He made the human race with the power of thought and of choosing the truth and doing right, so that all men are without excuse before God; for they have been born rational and contemplative. And if any one disbelieves that

---

[56] Thirlby remarks that the serpent was the symbol specially of eternity, of power, and of wisdom, and that there was scarcely any divine attribute to which the heathen did not find some likeness in this animal. See also Hardwick's *Christ and other Masters*, vol. ii, 146 (2nd ed.).

[57] [Note how he retaliates upon the calumny (cap. xxvi.) of the "upsetting of the lamp."]

[58] Literally, "For He foreknows some about to be saved by repentance, and some not yet perhaps born."

God cares for these things,[59] he will thereby either insinuate that God does not exist, or he will assert that though He exists He delights in vice, or exists like a stone, and that neither virtue nor vice are anything, but only in the opinion of men these things are reckoned good or evil. And this is the greatest profanity and wickedness.

CHAP. XXIX.—CONTINENCE OF CHRISTIANS.

And again [we fear to expose children], lest some of them be not picked up, but die, and we become murderers. But whether we marry, it is only that we may bring up children; or whether we decline marriage, we live continently. And that you may understand that promiscuous intercourse is not one of our mysteries, one of our number a short time ago presented to Felix the governor in Alexandria a petition, craving that permission might be given to a surgeon to make him an eunuch. For the surgeons there said that they were forbidden to do this without the permission of the governor. And when Felix absolutely refused to sign such a permission, the youth remained single, and was satisfied with his own approving conscience, and the approval of those who thought as he did. And it is not our of place, we think, to mention here Antinous, who was alive but lately, and whom all were prompt, through fear, to worship as a god, though they knew both who he was and what was his origin.[60]

---

[59] Those things which concern the salvation of man; so Trollope and the other interpreters, except Otto, who reads τούτων masculine, and understands it of the men first spoken of. [See Plato (*Di Legibus*, opp. ix. p. 98, Bipont., 1786), and the valuable edition of Book X. by Professor Tayler Lewis (p. 52. etc.), New York, 1845.]

[60] For a sufficient account of the infamous history here alluded to and the extravagant grief of Hadrian, and the servility of the people, see Smith's *Dictionary of Biography:* "Antinous." [Note, "all were prompt, *through fear*," etc. Thus we may measure the defiant intrepidity of this stinging

CHAP. XXX.—WAS CHRIST NOT A MAGICIAN?

But lest any one should meet us with the question, What should prevent that He whom we call Christ, being a man born of men, performed what we call His mighty works by magical art, and by this appeared to be the Son of God? we will now offer proof, not trusting mere assertions, but being of necessity persuaded by those who prophesied [of Him] before these things came to pass, for with our own eyes we behold things that have happened and are happening just as they were predicted; and this will, we think, appear even to you the strongest and truest evidence.

CHAP. XXXI.—OF THE HEBREW PROPHETS.

There were, then among the Jews certain men who were prophets of God, through whom the prophetic Spirit published beforehand things that were to come to pass, ere ever they happened to be reigning among the Jews at the several times carefully preserved in their possession, when they had been arranged in books by the prophets themselves in their own Hebrew language. And when Ptolemy king of Egypt formed a library, and endeavoured to collect the writings of all men, he heard also of these prophets, and sent to Herod, who was at that time king of the Jews,[61] requesting that the books of the prophets be sent to him. And Herod the king did indeed send them, written, as they were, in the foresaid Hebrew language. And when their contents were found to be unintelligible to the Egyptians, he again sent and requested that men be commissioned to translate them into

sarcasm addressed to the "philosophers," with whose sounding titles this Apology begins.]

[61] Some attribute this blunder in chronology to Justin, others to his transcribers; it was Eleazar the high priest to whom Ptolemy applied.

the Greek language. And when this was done, the books remained with the Egyptians, where they are until now. They are also in the possession of all Jews throughout the world; but they, though they read, do not understand what is said, but count us foes and enemies; and, like yourselves, they kill and punish us whenever they have the power, as you can well believe. For in the Jewish war which lately raged, Barchochebas, the leader of the revolt of the Jews, gave orders that Christians alone should be led to cruel punishments, unless they would deny Jesus Christ and utter blasphemy. In these books, then, of the prophets we found Jesus our Christ foretold as coming, born of a virgin, growing up to man's estate, and healing every disease and every sickness, and raising the dead, and being hated, and unrecognized, and crucified, and dying, and rising again, and ascending into heaven, and being, and being called, the Son of God. We find it also predicted that certain persons should be sent by Him into every nation to publish these things, and that rather among the Gentiles [than among the Jews] men should believe on Him. And He was predicted before He appeared, first 5000 years before, and again 3000, then 2000, then 1000, and yet again 800; for in the succession of generations prophets after prophets arose.

CHAP. XXXII.—CHRIST PREDICTED BY MOSES.

Moses then, who was the first of the prophets, spoke in these words: "The scepter shall not depart from Judah, nor a lawgiver from between his feet, until He come for whom it is reserved; and He shall be the desire of the nations, binding His foal to the vine, washing His robe in the blood of the grape."[62] It is yours to make accurate inquiry, and ascertain up to whose time the Jews had a lawgiver and king of their

---

[62] Gen. xlix. 10.

own. Up to the time of Jesus Christ, who taught us, and interpreted the prophecies which were not yet understood, [they had a lawgiver] as was foretold by the holy and divine Spirit of prophecy through Moses, "that a ruler would not fail the Jews until He should come for whom the kingdom was reserved" (for Judah was the forefather of the Jews, from whom also they have their name of Jews); and after He (i.e., Christ) appeared, you began to rule the Jews, and gained possession of all their territory. And the prophecy, "He shall be the expectation of the nations," signified that there would be some of all nations who should look for Him to come again. And this indeed you can see for yourselves, and be convinced of by fact. For of all races of men there are some who look for Him who was crucified in Judæa, and after whose crucifixion the land was straightway surrendered to you as spoil of war. And the prophecy, "binding His foal to the vine, and washing His robe in the blood of the grape," was a significant symbol of the things that were to happen to Christ, and of what He was to do. For the foal of an ass stood bound to a vine at the entrance of a village, and He ordered His acquaintances to bring it to Him then; and when it was brought, He mounted and sat upon it, and entered Jerusalem, where was the vast temple of the Jews which was afterwards destroyed by you. And after this He was crucified, that the rest of the prophecy might be fulfilled. For this "washing His robe in the blood of the grape" was predictive of the passion He was to endure, cleansing by His blood those who believe on Him. For what is called by the Divine Spirit through the prophet "His robe," are those men who believe in Him in whom abideth the seed[63] of God, the Word. And what is spoken of as "the blood of the grape," signifies that He who should appear would have blood, though not of the seed of

---

[63] Grabe would here read, not σπέρμα, but πνεῦμα, the spirit; but the Benedictine, Otto, and Trollope all think that no change should be made.

man, but of the power of God. And the first power after God the Father and Lord of all is the Word, who is also the Son; and of Him we will, in what follows, relate how He took flesh and became man. For as man did not make the blood of the vine, but God, so it was hereby intimated that the blood should not be of human seed, but of divine power, as we have said above. And Isaiah, another prophet, foretelling the same things in other words, spoke thus: "A star shall rise out of Jacob, and a flower shall spring from the root of Jesse; and His arm shall the nations trust."[64] And a star of light has arisen, and a flower has sprung from the root of Jesse—this Christ. For by the power of God He was conceived by a virgin of the seed of Jacob, who was the father of Judah, who, as we have shown, was the father of the Jews; and Jesse was His forefather according to the oracle, and He was the son of Jacob and Judah according to lineal descent.

CHAP. XXXIII.—MANNER OF CHRIST'S BIRTH PREDICTED.

And hear again how Isaiah in express words foretold that He should be born of a virgin; for he spoke thus: "Behold, a virgin shall conceive, and bring forth a son, and they shall say for His name, 'God with us.'"[65] For things which were incredible and seemed impossible with men, these God predicted by the Spirit of prophecy as about to come to pass, in order that, when they came to pass, there might be no unbelief, but faith, because of their prediction. But lest some, not understanding the prophecy now cited, should charge us with the very things we have been laying to the charge of the poets who say that Jupiter went in to women through lust, let us try to explain the words. This, then, "Behold, a virgin

---

[64] Isa. xi. 1.
[65] Isa. vii. 14.

shall conceive," signifies that a virgin should conceive without intercourse. For if she had had intercourse with any one whatever, she was no longer a virgin; but the power of God having come upon the virgin, overshadowed her, and caused her while yet a virgin to conceive. And the angel of God who was sent to the same virgin at that time brought her good news, saying, "Behold, thou shalt conceive of the Holy Ghost, and shalt bear a Son, and He shall be called the Son of the Highest, and thou shalt call His name Jesus; for He shall save His people from their sins,"[66]—as they who have recorded all that concerns our Saviour Jesus Christ have taught, whom we believed, since by Isaiah also, whom we have now adduced, the Spirit of prophecy declared that he should be born as we intimated before. It is wrong, therefore, to understand the Spirit and the power of God as anything else that the Word, who is also the first-born of God, as the foresaid prophet Moses declared; and it was this which, when it came upon the virgin and overshadowed her, caused her to conceive, not by intercourse, but by power. And the name of Jesus in the Hebrew language means Σωτήρ (Saviour) in the Greek tongue. Wherefore, too, the angel said to the virgin, "Thou shalt call His name Jesus, for He shall save His people from their sins." And that the prophets are inspired[67] by no other than the Divine Word, even you, as I fancy, will grant.

CHAP. XXXIV.—PLACE OF CHRIST'S BIRTH FORETOLD.

And hear what part of earth He was to be born in, as another prophet, Micah, foretold. He spoke thus: "And thou,

---

[66] Luke i. 32; Matt. i. 21.

[67] θεοφοῦνται, lit. are borne by a god—a word used of those who were supposed to be wholly under the influence of a deity.

Bethlehem, the land of Judah, art not the least among the princes of Judah; for out of thee shall come forth a Governor, who shall feed My people."[68] Now there is a village in the land of the Jews, thirty-five stadia from Jerusalem, in which Jesus Christ was born, as you can ascertain also from the registers of the taxing made under Cyrenius, your first procurator in Judæa.

CHAP. XXXV.—OTHER FULFILLED PROPHECIES.

And how Christ after He was born was to escape notice of other men until He grew to man's estate, which also came to pass, hear what was foretold regarding this. There are the following predictions:[69]—"Unto us a child is born, and unto us a young man is given, and the government shall be upon His shoulders;"[70] which is significant of the power of the cross, for to it, when He was crucified, He applied His shoulders, as shall be more clearly made out in the ensuing discourse. And again the same prophet Isaiah, being inspired by the prophetic Spirit, said, "I have spread out my hands to a disobedient and gainsaying people, to those who walk in a way that is not good. They now ask of me judgment, and dare to draw near to God."[71] And again in other words, through another prophet, He says, "They pierced My hands and My feet, and for My vesture they cast lots."[72] And indeed David, the king and prophet, who uttered these things, suffered none of them; but Jesus Christ stretched

---

[68] Micah v. 2.

[69] These predictions have so little reference to the point Justin intends to make out, that some editors have supposed that a passage has here been lost. Others think the irrelevancy an insufficient ground for such a supposition. [See below, cap. xl.]

[70] Isa. ix. 6.

[71] Isa. lxv. 2, lviii. 2.

[72] Ps. xxii. 16

forth His hands, being crucified by the Jews speaking against Him, and denying that He was the Christ. And as the prophet spoke, they tormented Him, and set Him on the judgment-seat, and said, Judge us. And the expression, "They pierced my hands and my feet," was used in reference to the nails of the cross which were fixed in His hands and feet. And after He was crucified they cast lots upon His vesture, and they that crucified Him parted it among them. And that these things did happen, you can ascertain from the Acts of Pontius Pilate.[73] And we will cite the prophetic utterances of another prophet, Zephaniah,[74] to the effect that He was foretold expressly as to sit upon the foal of an ass and to enter Jerusalem. The words are these: "Rejoice greatly, O daughter of Zion; shout, O daughter of Jerusalem: behold, thy King cometh unto thee; lowly, and riding upon an ass, and upon a colt the foal of an ass."[75]

CHAP. XXXVI.—DIFFERENT MODES OF PROPHECY.

But when you hear the utterances of the prophets spoken as it were personally, you must not suppose that they are spoken by the inspired themselves, but by the Divine Word who moves them. For sometimes He declares things that are to come to pass, in the manner of one who foretells the future; sometimes He speaks as from the person of God the

---

[73] ἄκτων. These Acts of Pontius Pilate, or regular accounts of his procedure sent by Pilate to the Emperor Tiberius, are supposed to have been destroyed at an early period, possibly in consequence of the unanswerable appeal which the Christians constantly made to them. There exists a forgery in imitation of these Acts. See Trollope.

[74] The reader will notice that these are not the words of Zephaniah, but of Zechariah (ix. 9.), to whom also Justin himself refers them in the *Dial. Tryph*, c. 53. [Might be corrected in the text, therefore, as a clerical slip of the pen.]

[75] Zech. ix. 9.

Lord and Father of all; sometimes as from the person of the people answering the Lord or His Father, just as you can see even in your own writers, one man being the writer of the whole, but introducing the persons who converse. And this the Jews who possessed the books of the prophets did not understand, and therefore did not recognize Christ even when He came, but even hate us who say that He has come, and who prove that, as was predicted, He was crucified by them.

CHAP. XXXVII.—UTTERANCES OF THE FATHER.

And that this too may be clear to you, there were spoken from the person of the Father, through Isaiah the prophet, the following words: "The ox knoweth his owner, and the ass his master's crib; but Israel doth not know, and My people hath not understood. Woe, sinful nation, a people full of sins, a wicked seed, children that are transgressors, ye have forsaken the Lord."[76] And again elsewhere, when the same prophet speaks in like manner from the person of the Father, "What is the house that ye will build for Me? saith the Lord. The heaven is My throne, and the earth is My footstool."[77] And again, in another place, "Your new moons and your Sabbaths My soul hateth; and the great day of the fast and of ceasing from labour I cannot away with; nor, if ye come to be seen of Me, will I hear you: your hands are full of blood; and if ye bring fine flour, incense, it is abomination unto Me: the fat of lambs and the blood of bulls I do not desire. For who hath required this at your hands? But loose every bond of wickedness, tear asunder the tight knots of violent contracts, cover the houseless and naked, deal thy bread to

---

[76] Isa. i. 3. This quotation varies only in one word from that of the LXX.
[77] Isa. lxvi. 1.

the hungry."[78] What kind of things are taught through the prophets from [the person of] God, you can now perceive.

CHAP. XXXVIII.—UTTERANCES OF THE SON.

And when the Spirit of prophecy speaks from the person of Christ, the utterances are of this sort: "I have spread out My hands to a disobedient and gainsaying people, to those who walk in a way that is not good."[79] And again: "I gave My back to the scourges, and My cheeks to the buffetings; I turned not away My face from the shame of spittings; and the Lord was My helper: therefore was I not confounded: but I set My face as a firm rock; and I knew that I should not be ashamed, for He is near that justifieth Me."[80] And again, when He says, "They cast lots upon My vesture, and pierced My hands and My feet. And I lay down and slept, and rose again, because the Lord sustained Me."[81] And again, when He says, "They spake with their lips, they wagged the head, saying, Let Him deliver Himself."[82] And that all these things happened to Christ at the hands of the Jews, you can ascertain. For when He was crucified, they did shoot out the lip, and wagged their heads, saying, "let Him who raised the dead save Himself."[83]

CHAP. XXXIX.—DIRECT
PREDICTIONS BY THE SPIRIT.

And when the Spirit of prophecy speaks as predicting things that are to come to pass, He speaks in this way: "For

---

[78] Isa. i. 14, xviii. 6.
[79] Isa. lxv. 2.
[80] Isa. l. 6.
[81] Ps. xxii. 13, iii. 5.
[82] Ps. xxii. 7.
[83] Comp. Matt. xxvii. 39.

out of Zion shall go forth the law, and the word of the Lord from Jerusalem. And He shall judge among the nations, and shall rebuke many people; and they shall beat their swords into ploughshares, and their spears into pruning-hooks: nation shall not lift up sword against nation, neither shall they learn way any more."[84] And that it did so come to pass, we can convince you. For from Jerusalem there went out into the world, men, twelve in number, and these illiterate, of no ability in speaking: but by the power of God they proclaimed to every race of men that they were sent by Christ to teach to all the word of God; and we who formerly used to murder one another do not only now refrain from making war upon our enemies, but also, that we may not lie nor deceive our examiners, willingly die confessing Christ. For that saying, "The tongue has sworn but the mind is unsworn,"[85] might be imitated by us in this matter. But if the soldiers enrolled by you, and who have taken the military oath, prefer their allegiance to their own life, and parents, and country, and all kindred, though you can offer them nothing incorruptible, it were verily ridiculous if we, who earnestly long for incorruption, should not endure all things, in order to obtain what we desire from Him who is able to grant it.

CHAP. XL.—CHRIST'S ADVENT FORETOLD.

And hear how it was foretold concerning those who published His doctrine and proclaimed His appearance, the above-mentioned prophet and king speaking thus by the Spirit of prophecy: "Day unto day uttereth speech, and night unto night showeth knowledge. There is no speech nor language where their voice is not heard. Their voice has gone out into all the earth, and their words to the ends of the

---

[84] Isa. ii. 3.
[85] Eurip., *Hipp.*, 608.

world. In the sun hath He set His tabernacle, and he as a bridegroom going out of his chamber shall rejoice as a giant to run his course."[86] And we have thought it right and relevant to mention some other prophetic utterances of David besides these; from which you may learn how the Spirit of prophecy exhorts men to live, and how He foretold the conspiracy which was formed against Christ by Herod the king of the Jews, and the Jews themselves, and Pilate, who was your governor among them, with his soldiers; and how He should be believed on by men of every race; and how God calls Him His Son, and has declared that He will subdue all his enemies under Him; and how the devils, as much as they can, strive to escape the power of God the Father and Lord of all, and the power of Christ Himself; and how God calls all to repentance before the day of judgment comes. These things were uttered thus: "Blessed is the man who hath not walked in the counsel of the ungodly, nor stood in the way of sinners, nor sat in the seat of the scornful: but his delight is in the law of the Lord; and in His law will he meditate day and night. And he shall be like a tree planted by the rivers of waters, which shall give his fruit in his season; and his leaf shall not wither, and whatsoever he doeth shall prosper. The ungodly are not so, but are like the chaff which the wind driveth away from the face of the earth. Therefore the ungodly shall not stand in the judgment, nor sinners in the council of the righteous; but the way of the ungodly shall perish. Why do the heathen rage, and the people imagine new things? The kings of the earth set themselves, and the rulers take counsel together, against the Lord, and against His Anointed, saying, Let us break their bands asunder, and

---

[86] Ps. xix. 2. etc. [Note how J. excuses himself for the apparent irrelevancy of some of his citations (cap. xxxv., note), though quite in the manner of Plato himself. These Scriptures were of novel interest, and he was stimulating his readers to study the Septuagint.]

cast their yoke from us. He that dwelleth in the heavens shall laugh at them, and the Lord shall have them in derision. Then shall He speak to them in His wrath, and vex them in His sore displeasure. yet have I been set by Him a King on Zion His holy hill, declaring the decree of the Lord. The Lord said to Me, Thou art My Son; this day have I begotten Thee. Ask of Me, and I shall give Thee the heathen for Thine inheritance, and the uttermost parts of the earth as Thy possession. Thou shalt herd them with a rod of iron; as the vessels of a potter shalt Thou dash them in pieces. Be wise now, therefore, O ye kings; be instructed, all ye judges of the earth. Serve the Lord with fear, and rejoice with trembling. Embrace instruction, lest at any time the Lord be angry, and ye perish from the right way, when His wrath has been suddenly kindled. Blessed are all they that put their trust in Him."[87]

CHAP. XLI.—THE CRUCIFIXION PREDICTED.

And again, in another prophecy, the Spirit of prophecy, through the same David, intimated that Christ, after He had been crucified, should reign, and spoke as follows: "Sing to the Lord, all the earth, and day by day declare His salvation. For great is the Lord, and greatly to be praised, to be feared above all the gods. For all the gods of the nations are idols of devils; but God made the heavens. Glory and praise are before His face, strength and glorying are in the habitation of His holiness. Give Glory to the Lord, the Father everlasting. Receive grace, and enter his presence, and worship in His holy courts. Let all the earth fear before His face; let it be

---

[87] Ps. i. ii.

established, and not shaken. Let them rejoice among the nations. The Lord hath reigned from the tree."[88]

CHAP. XLII.—PROPHECY USING THE PAST TENSE.

But when the Spirit of prophecy speaks of things that are about to come to pass as if they had already taken place,—as may be observed even in the passages already cited by me,— that this circumstance may afford no excuse to readers [for misinterpreting them], we will make even this also quite plain. The things which He absolutely knows will take place, He predicts as if already they had taken place. And the utterances must be thus received, you will perceive, if you give your attention to them. The words cited above, David uttered 1500[89] years before Christ became a man and was crucified; and no one of those who lived before Him, nor yet of His contemporaries, afforded joy to the Gentiles by being crucified. But our Jesus Christ, being crucified and dead, rose again, and having ascended to heaven, reigned; and by those things which were published in His name among all nations by the apostles, there is joy afforded to those who expect the immortality promised by Him.

CHAP. XLIII.—RESPONSIBILITY ASSERTED.

But lest some suppose, from what has been said by us, that we say that whatever happens, happens by a fatal necessity, because it is foretold as known beforehand, this

---

[88] Ps. xcvi. 1. etc. This last clause, which is not extant in our copies, either of the LXX. or of the Hebrew, Justin charged the Jews with erasing. See *Dial. Tryph.*, c. 73. [Concerning the eighteen Jewish alterations, see *Pearson on the Creed*, art. iv. p. 335. Ed. London, 1824.]

[89] A chronological error, whether of the copyist or of Justin himself cannot be known.

too we explain. We have learned from the prophets, and we hold it to be true, that punishments, and chastisements, and good rewards, are rendered according to the merit of each man's actions. Since if it be not so, but all things happen by fate, neither is anything at all in our own power. For if it be fated that this man, e.g., be good, and this other evil, neither is the former meritorious nor the latter to be blamed. And again, unless the human race have the power of avoiding evil and choosing good by free choice, they are not accountable for their actions, of whatever kind they be. But that it is by free choice they both walk uprightly and stumble, we thus demonstrate. We see the same man making a transition to opposite things. Now, if it had been fated that he were to be either good or bad, he could never have been capable of both the opposites, nor of so many transitions. But not even would some be good and others bad, since we thus make fate the cause of evil, and exhibit her as acting in opposition to herself; or that which has been already stated would seem to be true, that neither virtue nor vice is anything, but that things are only reckoned good or evil by opinion; which, as the true word shows, is the greatest impiety and wickedness. But this we assert is inevitable fate, that they who choose the good have worthy rewards, and they who choose the opposite have their merited awards. For not like other things, as trees and quadrupeds, which cannot act by choice, did God make man: for neither would he be worthy of reward or praise did he not of himself choose the good, but were created for this end;[90] nor, if he were evil, would be worthy of punishment, not being evil of himself, but being able to be nothing else than what he was made.

---

[90] Or, "but were made so." The words are, ἀλλά τοῦτο γνόμενοςand the meaning of Justin is sufficiently clear.

CHAP. XLIV.—NOT NULLIFIED BY PROPHECY.

And the holy Spirit of prophecy taught us this, telling us by Moses that God spoke thus to the man first created: "Behold, before thy face are good and evil: choose the good."[91] And again, by the other prophet Isaiah, that the following utterance was made as if from God the Father and Lord of all: "Wash you, make you clean; put away evils from your souls; learn to do well; judge the orphan, and plead for the widow: and come and let us reason together, saith the Lord: And if your sins be as scarlet, I will make them white as wool; and if they be red like as crimson, I will make them while as snow. And if ye be willing and obey Me, ye shall eat the good of the land; but if ye do not obey Me, the sword shall devour you: for the mouth of the Lord hath spoken it."[92] And that expression, "The sword shall devour you," does not mean that the disobedient shall be slain by the sword, but the sword of God is fire, of which they who choose to do wickedly become the fuel. Wherefore He says, "The sword shall devour you: for the mouth of the Lord hath spoken it." And if He had spoken concerning a sword that cuts and at once dispatches, He would not have said, shall *devour*. And so, too, Plato, when he says, "The blame is his who chooses, and God is blameless,"[93] took this from the prophet Moses and uttered it. For Moses is more ancient than all the Greek writers. And whatever both philosophers and poets have said concerning the immortality of the soul, or punishments after death, or contemplation of things heavenly, or doctrines of the like kind, they have received such suggestions from the prophets as have enabled them to

---

[91] Deut. xxx. 15, 19.

[92] Isa. i. 16, etc.

[93] Plato, Rep. x. [On this remarkable passage refer to Biog. Note above. See, also, brilliant note of the sophist De Maistre, (*Euvres*, ii. p. 105. Ed. Paris, 1853.]

understand and interpret these things. And hence there seem to be seed of truth among all men; but they are charged with not accurately understanding [the truth] when they assert contradictories. So that what we say about future events being foretold, we do not say it as if they came about by a fatal necessity; but God foreknowing all that shall be done by all men, and it being His decree that the future actions of men shall all be recompensed according to their several value, He foretells by the Spirit of prophecy that He will bestow meet rewards according to the merit of the actions done, always urging the human race to effort and recollection, showing that He cares and provides for men. But by the agency of the devils death has been decreed against those who read the books of Hystaspes, or of the Sibyl,[94] or of the prophets, that through fear they may prevent men who read them from receiving the knowledge of the good, and may retain them in slavery to themselves; which, however, they could not always effect. For not only do we fearlessly read them, but as you see, bring them for your inspection, knowing that their contents will be pleasing to all. And if we persuade even a few, our gain will be very great; for, as good husbandmen, we shall receive the reward from the Master.

CHAP. XLV.—CHRIST'S SESSION IN HEAVEN FORETOLD.

And that God the Father of all would bring Christ to heaven after He had raised Him from the dead, and would keep Him there[95] until He has subdued His enemies the

---

[94] [On the Orphica and Sibyllina, see Bull, W[indiscernible], vol. vi. pp. 291-298.]

[95] So Thirlby, Otto, and Trollope seem all to understand the word πατέχειν: yet it seems worth considering whether Justin has not borrowed both the sense and the word from 2 Thess. ii. 6, 7.

devils, and until the number of those who are foreknown by Him as good and virtuous is complete, on whose account He has still delayed the consummation—hear what was said by the prophet David. These are his words: "The Lord said unto My Lord, Sit Thou at My right hand, until I make Thine enemies Thy footstool. The Lord shall send to Thee the rod of power out of Jerusalem; and rule Thou in the midst of Thine enemies. With Thee is the government in the day of Thy power, in the beauties of Thy saints: from the womb of morning[96] have I begotten Thee."[97] That which he says, "He shall send to Thee the rod of power out of Jerusalem," is predictive of the mighty word, which His apostles, going forth from Jerusalem, preached everywhere; and though death is decree against those who teach or at all confess the name of Christ, we everywhere both embrace and teach it. And if you also read these words in a hostile spirit, ye can do no more, as I said before, than kill us; which indeed does no harm to us, but to you and all who unjustly hate us, and do not repent, brings eternal punishment by fire.

CHAP. XLVI.—THE WORD IN THE WORLD BEFORE CHRIST.

But lest some should, without reason, and for the perversion of what we teach, maintain that we say that Christ was born one hundred and fifty years ago under Cyrenius, and subsequently, in the time of Pontius Pilate, taught what we say He taught; and should cry out against us as though all men who were born before Him were irresponsible—let us anticipate and solve the difficulty. We have been taught that Christ is the first-born of God, and we have declared above that He is the Word of whom every race of men were

---

[96] Or, "before the morning star."
[97] Ps. cx. 1, etc.

partakers; and those who lived reasonably[98] are Christians, even though they have been thought atheists; as, among the Greeks, Socrates and Heraclitus, and men like them; and among the barbarians, Abraham, and Ananias, and Azarias, and Misael, and Elias, and many others whose actions and names we now decline to recount, because we know it would be tedious. So that even they who lived before Christ, and lived without reason, were wicked and hostile to Christ, and slew those who lived reasonably. But who, through the power of the Word, according to the will of God the Father and Lord of all, He was born of a virgin as a man, and was named Jesus, and was crucified, and died, and rose again, and ascended into heaven, an intelligent man will be able to comprehend from what has been already so largely said. And we, since the proof of this subject is less needful now, will pass for the present to the proof of those things which are urgent.

CHAP. XLVII.—DESOLATION OF JUDÆA FORETOLD.

That the land of the Jews, then, was to be laid waste, hear what was said by the Spirit of prophecy. And the words were spoken as if from the person of the people wondering at what had happened. They are these: "Sion is a wilderness, Jerusalem a desolation. The house of our sanctuary has become a curse, and the glory which our fathers blessed is burned up with fire, and all its glorious things are laid waste: and Thou refrainest Thyself at these things, and hast held Thy peace, and hast humbled us very sore."[99] And ye are

---

[98] μετά λόγου, "with reason," or "the Word." [This remarkable passage on the salvability and accountability of the heathen is noteworthy. See, on St. Matt. xxv. 32, *Morsels of Criticism* by the eccentric but thoughtful Ed. King, p. 341. London, 1788].

[99] Isa. lxiv. 10-12.

convinced that Jerusalem has been laid waste, as was predicted. And concerning its desolation, and that no one should be permitted to inhabit it, there was the following prophecy by Isaiah: "Their land is desolate, their enemies consume it before them, and none of them shall dwell therein."[100] And that it is guarded by you lest any one dwell in it, and that death is decreed against a Jew apprehended entering it, you know very well.[101]

CHAP. XLVIII.—CHRIST'S WORK AND DEATH FORETOLD.

And that it was predicted that our Christ should heal all diseases and raise the dead, hear what was said. There are these words: "At His coming the lame shall leap as an hart, and the tongue of the stammerer shall be clear speaking: the blind shall see, and the lepers shall be cleansed; and the dead shall rise, and walk about."[102] And that He did those things, you can learn from the Acts of Pontius Pilate. And how it was predicted by the Spirit of prophecy that He and those who hoped in Him should be slain, hear what was said by Isaiah. These are the words: "Behold now the righteous perisheth, and no man layeth it to heart; and just men are taken away, and no man considereth. From the presence of wickedness is the righteous man taken, and his burial shall be in peace: he is taken from our midst."[103]

---

[100] Isa. i. 7.
[101] [*Ad hominem*, referring to the cruel decree of Hadrian, which the philosophic Antomines did not annul.]
[102] Isa. xxxv. 6.
[103] Isa. lvii. 1.

CHAP. XLIX.—HIS REJECTION
BY THE JEWS FORETOLD.

And again, how it was said by the same Isaiah, that the Gentile nations who were not looking for Him should worship Him, but the Jews who always expected Him should not recognize Him when He came. And the words are spoken as from the person of Christ; and they are these: "I was manifest to them that asked not for Me; I was found of them that sought Me not: I said, Behold Me, to a nation that called not on My name. I spread out My hands to a disobedient and gainsaying people, to those who walked in a way that is not good, but follow after their own sins; a people that provoketh Me to anger to My face."[104] For the Jews having prophecies, and being always in expectation of the Christ to come, did not recognise Him; and not only so, but even treated Him shamefully. But the Gentiles, who had never heard anything about Christ, until the apostles set out from Jerusalem and preached concerning Him, and gave them the prophecies, were filled with joy and faith, and cast away their idols, and dedicated themselves to the Unbegotten God through Christ. And that it was foreknown that these infamous things should be uttered against those who confessed Christ, and that those who slandered Him, and said that it was well to preserve the ancient customs, should be miserable, hear what was briefly said by Isaiah; it is this: "Woe unto them that call sweet bitter, and bitter sweet."[105]

CHAP. L.—HIS HUMILIATION PREDICTED.

But that, having become man for our sakes, He endured to suffer and to be dishonoured, and that He shall come again

---

[104] Isa. lxv. 1-3.
[105] Isa. v. 20.

with glory, hear the prophecies which relate to this; they are these: "Because they delivered His soul unto death, and He was numbered with the transgressors, He has borne the sin of many, and shall make intercession for the transgressors. For, behold, My Servant shall deal prudently, and shall be exalted, and shall be greatly extolled. As many were astonished at Thee, so marred shall Thy form be before men, and so hidden from them Thy glory; so shall many nations wonder, and the kings shall shut their mouths at Him. For they to whom it was not told concerning Him, and they who have not heard, shall understand. O Lord, who hath believed our report? and to whom is the arm of the Lord revealed? We have declared before Him as a child, as a root in a dry ground. He had no form, nor glory; and we say Him, and there was no form nor comeliness: but His form was dishonoured and marred more than the sons of men. A man under the stroke, and knowing how to bear infirmity, because His face was turned away: He was despised, and of no reputation. It is He who bears our sins, and is afflicted for us; yet we did esteem Him smitten, stricken, and afflicted. But He was wounded for our transgressions, He was bruised for our iniquities, the chastisement of peace was upon Him, by His stripes we are healed. All we, like sheep, have gone astray; every man has wandered in his own way. And He delivered Him for our sins; and He opened not His mouth for all His affliction. He was brought as a sheep to the slaughter, and as a lamb before his shearer is dumb, so He openeth not His mouth. In His humiliation, His judgment was taken away."[106] Accordingly, after He was crucified, even all His acquaintances forsook Him, having denied Him; and afterwards, when He had risen from the dead and appeared to them, and had taught them to read the prophecies in which all these things were foretold as coming to pass, and when

---

[106] Isa. lii.13-15, liii. 1-8.

they had seen Him ascending into heaven, and had believed, and had received power sent thence by Him upon them, and went to every race of men, they taught these things, and were called apostles.

CHAP. LI.—THE MAJESTY OF CHRIST.

And that the Spirit of prophecy might signify to us that He who suffers these things has an ineffable origin, and rules His enemies, He spake thus: "His generation who shall declare? because His life is cut off from the earth: for their transgressions He comes to death. And I will give the wicked for His burial, and the rich for His death; because He did no violence, neither was any deceit in His mouth. And the Lord is pleased to cleanse Him from the stripe. If He be given for sin, your soul shall see His seed prolonged in days. And the Lord is pleased to deliver His soul from grief, to show Him light, and to form Him with knowledge, to justify the righteous who richly serveth many. And He shall bear our iniquities. Therefore He shall inherit many, and He shall divide the spoil of the strong; because His soul was delivered to death: and He was numbered with the transgressors; and He bare the sins of many, and He was delivered up for their transgressions."[107] Hear, too, how He was to ascend into heaven according to prophecy. It was thus spoken: "Lift up the gates of heaven; be ye opened, that the King of glory may come in. Who is this King of glory? The Lord, strong and mighty."[108] And how also He should come again out of heaven with glory, hear what was spoken in reference to this by the prophet Jeremiah.[109] His words are: "Behold, as the

---

[107] Isa. liii. 8-12.
[108] Ps. xxiv. 7.
[109] This prophecy occurs not in Jeremiah, but in Dan. vii. 13.

Son of man He cometh in the clouds of heaven, and His angels with Him."[110]

CHAP. LII.—CERTAIN FULFILLMENT OF PROPHECY.

Since, then, we prove that all things which have already happened had been predicted by the prophets before they came to pass, we must necessarily believe also that those things which are in like manner predicted, but are yet to come to pass, shall certainly happen. For as the things which have already taken place came to pass when foretold, and even though unknown, so shall the things that remain, even though they be unknown and disbelieved, yet come to pass. For the prophets have proclaimed two advents of His: the one, that which is already past, when He came as a dishonoured and suffering Man; but the second, when, according to prophecy, He shall come from heaven with glory, accompanied by His angelic host, when also He shall raise the bodies of all men who have lived, and shall clothe those of the worthy with immortality, and shall send those of the wicked, endued with eternal sensibility, into everlasting fire with the wicked devils. And that these things also have been foretold as yet to be, we will prove. By Ezekiel the prophet it was said: "Joint shall be joined to joint, and bone to bone, and flesh shall grow again; and every knee shall bow to the Lord, and every tongue shall confess Him."[111] And in what kind of sensation and punishment the wicked are to be, hear from what was said in like manner with reference to this; it is as follows: "Their worm shall not rest, and their fire shall not be quenched;"[112] and then shall they

---

[110] Dan. vii. 13.
[111] Ezek. xxxvii. 7, 8; Isa. xlv. 24.
[112] Isa. lxvi. 24.

repent, when it profits them not. And what the people of the Jews shall say and do, when they see Him coming in glory, has been thus predicted by Zechariah the prophet: "I will command the four winds to gather the scattered children; I will command the north wind to bring them, and the south wind, that it keep not back. And then in Jerusalem there shall be great lamentation, not the lamentation of mouths or of lips, but the lamentation of the heart; and they shall rend not their garments, but their hearts. Tribe by tribe they shall mourn, and then they shall look on Him whom they have pierced; and they shall say, Why, O Lord, hast Thou made us to err from Thy way? The glory which our fathers blessed, has for us been turned into shame."[113]

CHAP. LIII.—SUMMARY OF THE PROPHECIES.

Though we could bring forward many other prophecies, we forbear, judging these sufficient for the persuasion of those who have ears to hear and understand; and considering also that those persons are able to see that we do not make mere assertions without being able to produce proof, like those fables that are told of the so-called sons of Jupiter. For with what reason should we believe of a crucified man that He is the first-born of the unbegotten God, and Himself will pass judgment on the whole human race, unless we had found testimonies concerning Him published before He came and was born as man, and unless we say that things had happened accordingly—the devastation of the land of the Jews, and men of every race persuaded by His teaching through the apostles, and rejecting their old habits, in which, being deceived, they had had their conversation; yea, seeing ourselves too, and knowing that the Christians from among the Gentiles are both more numerous and more true than

---

[113] Zech. xii. 3-14; Isa. lxiii. 17, lxiv. 11.

those from among the Jews and Samaritans? For all the other human races are called Gentiles by the Spirit of prophecy; but the Jewish and Samaritan races are called the tribe of Israel, and the house of Jacob. And the prophecy in which it was predicted that there should be more believers from the Gentiles than from the Jews and Samaritans, we will produce: it ran thus: "Rejoice, O barren, thou that dost not bear; break forth and shout, thou that dost not travail, because many more are the children of the desolate than of her that hath an husband."[114] For all the Gentiles were "desolate" of the true God, serving the works of their hands; but the Jews and Samaritans, having the word of God delivered to them by the prophets, and always expecting the Christ, did not recognise Him when He came, except some few, of whom the Spirit of prophecy by Isaiah had predicted that they should be saved. He spoke as from their person: "Except the Lord had left us a seed, we should have been as Sodom and Gomorrah."[115] For Sodom and Gomorrah are related by Moses to have been cities of ungodly men, which God burned with fire and brimstone, and overthrew, no on e of their inhabitants being saved except a certain stranger, a Chaldæan by birth, whose name was Lot; with whom also his daughters were rescued. And those who care may yet see their whole country desolate and burned, and remaining barren. And to show how those from among the Gentiles were foretold as more true and more believing, we will cite what was said by Isaiah[116] the prophet; for he spoke as follows: "Israel is uncircumcised in heart, but the Gentiles are uncircumcised in the flesh." So many things therefore, as these, when they are seen with the eye, are enough to produce conviction and belief in those who embrace the

---

[114] Isa. liv. 1.
[115] Isa. i. 9.
[116] The following words are found, not in Isaiah, but in Jer. ix. 26.

truth, and are not bigoted in their opinions, nor are governed by their passions.

CHAP. LIV.—ORIGIN OF HEATHEN MYTHOLOGY.

But those who hand down myths which the poets have made, adduce no proof to the youths who learn them; and we proceed to demonstrate that they have been uttered by the influence of the wicked demons, to deceive and lead astray the human race. For having heard it proclaimed through the prophets that the Christ was to come, and that the ungodly among men were to be punished by fire, they put forward many to be called sons of Jupiter, under the impression that they would be able to produce in men the idea that the things which were said with regard to Christ were mere marvellous tales, like the things which were said by the poets. And these things were said both among the Greeks and among all nations where they [the demons] heard the prophets foretelling that Christ would specially be believed in; but that in hearing what was said by the prophets they did not accurately understand it, but imitated what was said of our Christ, like men who are in error, we will make plain. The prophet Moses, then, was, as we have already said, older than all writers: and by him, as we have also said before, it was thus predicted: "There shall not fail a prince from Judah, nor a lawgiver from between his feet, until He come for whom it is reserved; and He shall be the desire of the Gentiles, binding His foal to the vine, washing His robe in the blood of the grape."[117] The devils, accordingly, when they heard these prophetic words, said that Bacchus was the son of Jupiter, and gave out that he was the discoverer of the

---

[117] Gen. xlix. 10.

vine, and they number wine[118] [or, the ass] among his mysteries; and they taught that, having been torn in pieces, he ascended into heaven. And because in the prophecy of Moses it had not been expressly intimated whether He who was to come was the Son of God, and whether He would, riding on the foal, remain on earth or ascend into heaven, and because the name of "foal" could mean either the foal of an ass or the foal of a horse, they, not knowing whether He who was foretold would bring the foal of an ass or of a horse as the sign of His coming, nor whether He was the Son of God, as we said above, or of man, gave out that Bellerophon, a man born of man, himself ascended to heaven on his horse Pegasus. And when they heard it said by the other prophet Isaiah, that He should be born of a virgin, and by His own means ascend into heaven, they pretended that Perseus was spoken of. And when they knew what was said, as has been cited above, in the prophecies written aforetime, "Strong as a giant to run his course,"[119] they said that Hercules was strong, and had journeyed over the whole earth. And when, again, they learned that it had been foretold that He should heal every sickness, and raise the dead, the produced Æsculapius.

CHAP. LV.—SUMMARY OF THE PROPHECIES.

But in no instance, not even in any of those called sons of Jupiter, did they imitate the being crucified; for it was not understood by them, all the things said of it having been put symbolically.   And this, as the prophet foretold, is the

---

[118] In the MS the reading is οἶνον (wine): but as Justin's argument seems to require ὄνον (an ass), Sylburg inserted this latter word in his edition; and this reading is approved by Grabe and Thirlby, and adopted by Otto and Trollope. It may be added, that ἀναγράφουσι is much more suitable to ὄνον than to οἶνον.

[119] Ps. xix. 5.

greatest symbol of His power and rule; as is also proved by the things which fall under our observation. For consider all the things in the world, whether without this form they could be administered or have any community. For the sea is not traversed except that trophy which is called a sail abide safe in the ship; and the earth is not ploughed without it: diggers and mechanics do not their work, except with tools which have this shape. And the human form differs from that of the irrational animals in nothing else than in its being erect and having the hands extended, and having on the face extending from the forehead what is called the nose, through which there is respiration for the living creature; and this shows no other form than that of the cross. And so it was said by the prophet, "The breath before our face is the Lord Christ."[120] And the power of this form is shown by your own symbols on what are called "vexilla" [banners] and trophies, with which all your state possessions are made, using these as the insignia of your power and government, even though you do so unwittingly.[121] And with this form you consecrate the images of your emperors when they die, and you name them gods by inscriptions. Since therefore, we have urged you both by reason and by an evident form, and to the utmost of our ability, we know that now we are blameless even though you disbelieve; for our part is done and finished.

CHAP. LVI.—THE DEMONS STILL MISLEAD MEN.

But the evil spirits were not satisfied with saying, before Christ's appearance, that those who were said to be sons of Jupiter were born of him; but after He had appeared and been

---

[120] From Lam. iv. 20 (Sept.).

[121] [The Orientals delight in such refinements, but the "scandal of the cross" led the early Christians thus to retort upon the heathen; and the *Labarum* may have been the fruit of this very suggestion.]

born among men, and when they learned how He had been foretold by the prophets, and knew that He should be believed on and looked for by every nation, they again, as was said above, put forward other men, the Samaritans Simon and Menander, who did many mighty works by magic and deceived many, and still keep them deceived. For even among yourselves, as we said before,[122] Simon was in the royal city Rome in the reign of Claudius Cæsar, and so greatly astonished the sacred senate and people of the Romans, that he was considered a god, and honoured, like the others whom you honour as gods, with a statue. Wherefore we pray that the sacred senate and your people may, along with yourselves, be arbiters of this our memorial, in order that if any one be entangled by that man's doctrines, he may learn the truth, and so be able to escape error; and as for the statue, if you please, destroy it.

CHAP. LVII.—AND CAUSE PERSECUTION.

Nor can the devils persuade men that there will be no conflagration for the punishment of the wicked; as they were unable to effect that Christ should be hidden after He came. But this only can they effect, that they who live irrationally, and were brought up licentiously in wicked customs, and are prejudiced in their own opinions, should kill and hate us; whom we not only do not hate, but, as is proved, pity and endeavour to lead to repentance. For we do not fear death, since it is acknowledged we must surely die; and there is nothing new, but all things continue the same in this administration of things; and if satiety overtakes those who enjoy even one year of these things, they ought to give heed to our doctrines, that they may live eternally free both from suffering and from want. But if they believe that there is

---

[122] [See cap. xxvi. above, and note p.187, below.]

nothing after death, but declare that those who die pass into insensibility, then they become our benefactors when they set us free from sufferings and necessities of this life, and prove themselves to be wicked, and inhuman, and bigoted. For they kill us with no intention of delivering us, but cut us off that we may be deprived of life and pleasure.

CHAP. LVIII.—AND RAISE UP HERETICS.

And, as we said before, the devils put forward Marcion of Pontus, who is even now teaching men to deny that God is the maker of all things in heaven and on earth, and that the Christ predicted by the prophets is His Son, and preaches another god besides the Creator of all, and likewise another son. And this man many have believed, as if he alone knew the truth, and laugh at us, though they have no proof of what they say, but are carried away irrationally as lambs by a wolf, and become the prey of atheistical doctrines, and of devils. For they who are called devils attempt nothing else than to seduce men from God who made them, and from Christ His first-begotten; and those who are unable to raise themselves above the earth they have riveted, and do now rivet, to things earthly, and to the works of their own hands; but those who devote themselves to the contemplation of things divine, they secretly beat back; and if they have not a wise sober-mindedness, and a pure and passionless life, they drive them into godlessness.

CHAP. LIX.—PLATO'S OBLIGATION TO MOSES.

And that you may learn that it was from our teachers—we mean the account given through the prophets—that Plato borrowed his statement that God, having altered matter which was shapeless, made the world, hear the very words spoken through Moses, who, as above shown, was the first prophet, and of greater antiquity than the Greek writers; and through whom the Spirit of prophecy, signifying how and from what material God at first formed the world, spake thus: "In the beginning God created the heaven and the earth. And the earth was invisible and unfurnished, and darkness was upon the face of the deep; and the Spirit of God moved over the waters. And God said, Let there be light; and it was so." So that both Plato and they who agree with him, and we ourselves, have learned, and you also can be convinced, that by the word of God the whole world was made out of the substance spoken of before by Moses. And that which the poets call Erebus, we know was spoken of formerly by Moses.[123]

CHAP. LX.—PLATO'S DOCTRINE OF THE CROSS.

And the physiological discussion[124] concerning the Son of God in the *Timæus* of Plato, where he says, "He placed him crosswise[125] in the universe," he borrowed in like manner from Moses; for in the writings of Moses it is related how at that time, when the Israelites went out of Egypt and were in the wilderness, they fell in with poisonous beasts, both vipers and asps, and every kind of serpent, which slew the people; and that Moses, by the inspiration and influence of God, took brass, and made it into the figure of a cross, and set it in the holy tabernacle, and said to the people, "If ye look to this

---

[123] Comp. Deut. xxxii. 22.

[124] Literally, "that which is treated physiologically."

[125] He impressed him as a χιασμα, i.e., in the form of the letter χ upon the universe." Plato is speaking of the soul of the universe. [Timaeus, Opp., vol. ix. p. 314. And see note of Langus (p.37) on p. 113 of Grabe. Here crops out the Platonic philosopher speaking after the fashion of his contemporaries, perhaps to conciliate his sovereign. See Professor Jowett's Introduction to the *Timæus*, which will aid the students.]

figure and believe, ye shall be saved thereby."[126] And when this was done, it is recorded that the serpents died, and it is handed down that the people thus escaped death. Which things Plato reading, and not accurately understanding, and not apprehending that it was the figure of the cross, but taking it to be a placing crosswise, he said that the power next to the first God was placed crosswise in the universe. And as to his speaking of a third, he did this because he read, as we said above, that which was spoken by Moses, "that the Spirit of God moved over the waters." For he gives the second place to the Logos which is with God, who he said was placed crosswise in the universe; and the third place to the Spirit who was said to be borne upon the water, saying, "And the third around the third."[127] And hear how the Spirit of prophecy signified through Moses that there should be a conflagration. He spoke thus: "Everlasting fire shall descend, and shall devour to the pit beneath."[128] It is not, then, that we hold the same opinions as others, but that all speak in imitation of ours. Among us these things can be heard and learned from persons who do not even know the forms of the letters, who are uneducated and barbarous in speech, though wise and believing in mind; some, indeed, even maimed and deprived of eyesight; so that you may understand that these things are not the effect of human wisdom, but are uttered by the power of God.

CHAP. LXI.—CHRISTIAN BAPTISM.

I will also relate the manner in which we dedicated ourselves to God when we had been made new through Christ; lest, if we omit this, we seem to be unfair in the

---

[126] Num. xxi. 8.

[127] Τά δέ τριτα περί τόν τρίτον.

[128] Deut. xxxii. 22.

explanation we are making. As many as are persuaded and believe that what we teach and say is true, and undertake to be able to live accordingly, are instructed to pray and to entreat God with fasting, for the remission of their sins that are past, we praying and fasting with them. Then they are brought by us where there is water, and are regenerated in the same manner in which we were ourselves regenerated. For, in the name of God, the Father and Lord of the universe, and of our Saviour Jesus Christ, and of the Holy Spirit, they then receive the washing with water. For Christ also said, "Except ye be born again, ye shall not enter into the kingdom of heaven."[129] Now, that it is impossible for those who have once been born to enter into their mothers' wombs, is manifest to all. And how those who have sinned and repent shall escape their sins, is declared by Esaias the prophet, as I wrote above;[130] he thus speaks: "Wash you, make you clean; put away the evil of your doings from your souls; learn to do well; judge the fatherless, and plead for the widow: and come and let us reason together, saith the Lord. And though your sins be as scarlet, I will make them white like wool; and though they be as crimson, I will make them white as snow. But if ye refuse and rebel, the sword shall devour you: for the mouth of the Lord hath spoken it."[131]

And for this [rite] we have learned from the apostles this reason. Since at our birth we were born without our own knowledge or choice, by our parents coming together, and were brought up in bad habits and wicked training; in order that we may not remain the children of necessity and of ignorance, but may become the children of choice and knowledge, and may obtain in the water the remission of sins formerly committed, there is pronounced over him who

---

[129] John iii. 5.
[130] Chap. xliv.
[131] Isa. i. 16-20.

chooses to be born again, and has repented of his sins, the name of God the Father and Lord of the universe; he who leads to the laver the person that is to be washed calling him by this name alone. For no one can utter the name of the ineffable God; and if any one dare to say that there is a name, he raves with a hopeless madness. And this washing is called illumination, because they who learn these things are illuminated in their understandings. And in the name of Jesus Christ, who was crucified under Pontius Pilate, and in the name of the Holy Ghost, who through the prophets foretold all things about Jesus, he who is illuminated is washed.

CHAP. LXII.—ITS IMITATION BY DEMONS.

And the devils, indeed, having heard this washing published by the prophet, instigated those who enter their temples, and are about to approach them with libations and burnt-offerings, also to sprinkle themselves; and they cause them also to wash themselves entirely, as they depart [from the sacrifice], before they enter into the shrines in which their images are set. And the command, too, given by the priests to those who enter and worship in the temples, that they take off their shoes, the devils, learning what happened to the above-mentioned prophet Moses, have given in imitation of these things. For at that juncture, when Moses was ordered to go down into Egypt and lead out the people of the Israelites who were there, and while he was tending the flocks of his maternal uncle[132] in the land of Arabia, our Christ conversed with him under the appearance of fire from a bush, and said, "Put off thy shoes, and draw near and hear." And he, when he had put off his shoes and drawn near, heard that he was to go down into Egypt and lead out

---

[132] Thirlby conjectures that Justin here confused in his mind the histories of Moses and Jacob.

the people of the Israelites there; and he received mighty power from Christ, who spoke to him in the appearance of fire, and went down and led out the people, having done great and marvelous things; which, if you desire to know, you will learn them accurately from his writings.

CHAP. LXIII.—HOW GOD APPEARED TO MOSES.

And all the Jews even now teach that the nameless God spake to Moses; whence the Spirit of prophecy, accusing them by Isaiah the prophet mentioned above, said "The ox knoweth his owner, and the ass his master's crib; but Israel doth not know Me, and My people do not understand."[133] And Jesus the Christ, because the Jews knew not what the Father was, and what the Son, in like manner accused them; and Himself said, "No one knoweth the Father, but the Son; nor the Son, but the Father, and they to whom the Son revealeth Him."[134] Now the Word of God is His Son, as we have before said. And He is called Angel and Apostle; for He declares whatever we ought to know, and is sent forth to declare whatever is revealed; as our Lord Himself says, "He that heareth Me, heareth Him that sent Me."[135] From the writings of Moses also this will be manifest; for thus it is written in them, "And the Angel of God spake to Moses, in a flame of fire out of the bush, and said, I am that I am, the God of Abraham, the God of Isaac, the God of Jacob, the God of thy fathers; go down into Egypt, and bring forth My people."[136] And if you wish to learn what follows, you can do so from the same writings; for it is impossible to relate the whole here. But so much is written for the sake of

---

[133] Isa. i. 3.
[134] Matt. xi. 27.
[135] Luke x. 16.
[136] Ex. iii. 6.

proving that Jesus the Christ is the Son of God and His Apostle, being of old the Word, and appearing sometimes in the form of fire, and sometimes in the likeness of angels; but now, by the will of God, having become man for the human race, He endured all the sufferings which the devils instigated the senseless Jews to inflict upon Him; who, though they have it expressly affirmed in the writings of Moses, "And the angel of God spake to Moses in a flame of fire in a bush, and said, I am that I am, the God of Abraham, and the God of Isaac, and the God of Jacob," yet maintain that He who said this was the Father and Creator of the universe. Whence also the Spirit of prophecy rebukes them, and says, "Israel doth not know Me, my people have not understood Me."[137] And again, Jesus, as we have already shown, while He was with them, said, "No one knoweth the Father, but the Son; nor the Son but the Father, and those to whom the Son will reveal Him."[138] The Jews, accordingly, being throughout of opinion that it was the Father of the universe who spake to Moses, though He who spake to him was indeed the Son of God, who is called both Angel and Apostle, are justly charged, both by the Spirit of prophecy and by Christ Himself, with knowing neither the Father nor the Son. For they who affirm that the Son is the Father, are proved neither to have become acquainted with the Father, nor to know that the Father of the universe has a Son; who also, being the first-begotten Word of God, is even God. And of old He appeared in the shape of fire and in the likeness of an angel to Moses and to the other prophets; but now in the times of your reign,[139] having, as we before said, become Man by a virgin, according to the counsel of the Father, for the salvation of those who believe on Him, He endured both

---

[137] Isa. i. 3.
[138] Matt. xi. 27.
[139] [Rather, "of your empire."]

to be set at nought and to suffer, that by dying and rising again He might conquer death. And that which was said out of the bush to Moses, "I am that I am, the God of Abraham, and the God of Isaac, and the God of Jacob, and the God of your fathers,"[140] this signified that they, even though dead, are yet in existence, and are men belonging to Christ Himself. For they were the first of all men to busy themselves in the search after God; Abraham being the father of Isaac, and Isaac of Jacob, as Moses wrote.

CHAP. LXIV.—FURTHER MISREPRESENTATIONS OF THE TRUTH.

From what has been already said, you can understand how the devils, in imitation of what was said by Moses, asserted that Proserpine was the daughter of Jupiter, and instigated the people to set up an image of her under the name of Kore [Cora, i.e., the maiden or daughter] at the spring-heads. For, as we wrote above,[141] Moses said, "In the beginning God made the heaven and the earth. And the earth was without form and unfurnished: and the Spirit of God moved upon the face of the waters." In imitation, therefore, of what is here said of the Spirit of God moving on the waters, they said that Proserpine [or Cora] was the daughter of Jupiter.[142] And in like manner also they craftily feigned that Minerva was the daughter of Jupiter, not by sexual union, but, knowing that God conceived and made the world by the Word, they say that Minerva is the first conception [ἔννοια]; which we consider to be very absurd, bringing forward the form of the conception in a female shape. And in like manner the actions

---

[140] Ex. iii. 6.
[141] Chap. lix.
[142] And therefore caused her to preside over the waters, as above.

of those others who are called sons of Jupiter sufficiently condemn them.

CHAP. LXV.—ADMINISTRATION OF THE SACRAMENTS.

But we, after we have thus washed him who has been convinced and has assented to our teaching, bring him to the place where those who are called brethren are assembled, in order that we may offer hearty prayers in common for ourselves and for the baptized [illuminated] person, and for all others in every place, that we may be counted worthy, now that we have learned the truth, by our works also to be found good citizens and keepers of the commandments, so that we may be saved with an everlasting salvation. Having ended the prayers, we salute one another with a kiss.[143] There is then brought to the president of the brethren[144] bread and a cup of wine mixed with water; and he taking them, gives praise and glory to the Father of the universe, through the name of the Son and of the Holy Ghost, and offers thanks at considerable length for our being counted worthy to receive these things at His hands. And when he had concluded the prayers and thanksgivings, all the people present express their assent by saying Amen. This word Amen answers in the Hebrew language to γένοιτο [so be it]. And when the president has given thanks, and all the people have expressed their assent, those who are called by us

---

[143] The kiss of charity, the kiss of peace, or "the peace" (ἡ εἰρήνη), was enjoined by the Apostle Paul in his Epistles to the Corinthians, Thessalonians, and Romans, and thence passed into common Christian usage. It was continued in the Western Church, under regulations to prevent its abuse, until the thirteenth century. Stanley remarks (*Corinthians*, i. 414), " It is still continued in the worship of the Coptic Church."

[144] τῷ προεστῶτι τῶν ἀδελφῶν. This expression may quite legitimately be translated, " to that one of the brethren who was presiding."

deacons give to each of those present to partake of the bread and wine mixed with water over which the thanksgiving was pronounced, and to those who are absent they carry away a portion.

CHAP. LXVI.—OF THE EUCHARIST.

And this food is called among us Σύχαριστία[145] [the Eucharist], of which no one is allowed to partake but the man who believes that the things which we teach are true, and who has been washed with the washing that is for the remission of sins, and unto regeneration, and who is so living as Christ has enjoined. For not as common bread and common drink do we receive these; but in like manner as Jesus Christ our Saviour, having been made flesh by the Word of God, had both flesh and blood for our salvation, so likewise have we been taught that the food which is blessed by the prayer of His word, and from which our blood and flesh by transmutation are nourished, is the flesh and blood of that Jesus who was made flesh.[146] For the apostles, in

---

[145] Literally, thanksgiving. See Matt. xxvi. 27.

[146] This passage is claimed alike by Calvinists, Lutherans, and Romanists; and, indeed, the language is so inexact, that each party may plausibly maintain that their own opinion is advocated by it. [But the same might be said of the words of our Lord himself; and, if such widely separated Christians can all adopt this passage, who can be sorry?] The expression, "the prayer of His word," or of the word we have from Him, seems to signify the prayer pronounced over the elements, in imitation of our Lord's thanksgiving before breaking the bread. [I must dissent from the opinion that the language is "inexact:" he expresses himself naturally as one who believes it is bread, but yet not "common bread." So Gelasius, Bishop of Rome (A.D. 490), "By the sacraments we are made partakers of the divine nature, and yet the substance and nature of bread and wine do not cease to be in them." etc. (See the original in *Blugham's Antiquities*, book xv. cap. 5. See Chrysost., *Epistl ad. Carsarium*, tom. iii. p. 753. Ed Migne.) Those desirous to pursue this inquiry will find the Patristic authorities in *Histeria Transubstantionis Papalis*, etc., *Edidit* F. Meyrick, Oxford. 1858. The famous tractate of Ratranin (A. D. 840) was

memoirs composed by them, which are called Gospels, have thus delivered unto us what was enjoined upon them; that Jesus took bread, and when He had given thanks, said, "This do ye in remembrance of Me.[147] this is My body;" and that, after the same manner, having taken the cup and given thanks, He said, "This is my blood;" and gave it to them alone. Which the wicked devils have imitated in the mysteries of Mithras, commanding the same thing to be done. For, that bread and a cup of water are placed with certain incantations in the mystic rites of one who is being initiated, you either know or can learn.

CHAP. LXVII.—WEEKLY WORSHIP OF THE CHRISTIANS.

And we afterwards continually remind each other of these things. And the wealthy among us help the needy; and we always keep together; and for all things wherewith we are supplied, we bless the Maker of all through His Son Jesus Christ, and through the Holy Ghost. And on the day called Sunday,[148] all who live in cities or in the country gather together to one place, and the memoirs of the apostles or the writings of the prophets are read, as long as time permits; then, when the reader has ceased, the president verbally instructs, and exhorts to the imitation of these good things. Then we all rise together and pray, and, as we before said, when our prayer is ended, bread and wine and water are brought, and the president in like manner offers prayers and thanksgivings, according to his ability,[149] and the people

---

published at Oxford, 1838, with the homily of Ælfric (A.D. 960) in a cheap edition.]

[147] Luke xxii. 19.

[148] τή τοῦ ʽΗλιου λεγομένη ἡυερα.

[149] ὁση δύναμις αὐτῷ,--a phrase over which there has been much contention, but which seems to admit of no other meaning than that given

assent, saying Amen; and there is a distribution to each, and a participation of that over which thanks have been given,[150] and to those who are absent a portion is sent by the deacons. And they who are well to do, and willing, give what each thinks fit; and what is collected is deposited with the president, who succours the orphans and widows, and those who, through sickness or any other cause, are in want, and those who are in bonds, and the strangers sojourning among us, and in a word takes care of all who are in need. But Sunday is the day on which we all hold our common assembly, because it is the first day on which God, having wrought a change in the darkness and matter, made the world; and Jesus Christ our Saviour on the same day rose from the dead. For He was crucified on the day before that of Saturn (Saturday); and on the day after that of Saturn, which is the day of the Sun, having appeared to His apostles and disciples, He taught them these things, which we have submitted to you also for your consideration.

CHAP. LXVIII.—CONCLUSION.

And if these things seem to you to be reasonable and true, honour them; but if they seem nonsensical, despise them as nonsense, and do not decree death against those who have done no wrong, as you would against enemies. For we forewarn you, that you shall not escape the coming judgment of God, if you continue in your injustice; and we ourselves will invite you to do that which is pleasing to God. And

---

above. [No need of any "contention." Langus renders, *Pro virili sud*, and Grabe illustrates by reference to *Apost. Const.*, lib. viii. cap. 12. Our own learned translators render the same phrase (cap. xiii., above) "to the utmost of our power." some say this favours extemporary prayers, and the others object. Oh! what matter either way! We all sing hymns, "according to our ability."]

[150] Or, of the eucharistic elements.

though from the letter of the greatest and most illustrious Emperor Adrian, your father, we could demand that you order judgment to be given as we have desired, yet we have made this appeal and explanation, not on the ground of Adrian's decision, but because we know that what we ask is just. And we have subjoined the copy of Adrian's epistle, that you may know that we are speaking truly about this. And the following is the copy:—

EPISTLE OF ADRIAN[151]
IN BEHALF OF THE CHRISTIANS.

I have received the letter addressed to me by your predecessor Serenius Granianus, a most illustrious man; and this communication I am unwilling to pass over in silence, lest innocent persons be disturbed, and occasion be given to the informers for practising villany. Accordingly, if the inhabitants of your province will so far sustain this petition of theirs as to accuse the Christians in some court of law, I do not prohibit them from doing so. But I will not suffer them to make use of mere entreaties and outcries. For it is far more just, if any one desires to make an accusation, that you give judgment upon it. If, therefore, any one makes the accusation, and furnishes proof that the said men do anything contrary to the laws, you shall adjudge punishments in proportion to the offences. And this, by Hercules, you shall give special heed to, that if any man shall, through mere calumny, bring an accusation against any of these persons, you shall award to him more severe punishments in proportion to his wickedness.

---

[151] Addressed to Minucius Fundanus. [Generally credited as genuine.]

EPISTLE OF ANTONINUS
TO THE COMMON ASSEMBLY OF ASIA.[152]

The Emperor Cæsar Titus Ælius Adrianus Antoninus Augustus Pius, Supreme Pontiff, in the fifteenth year of his tribuneship, Consul for the third time, Father of the fatherland, to the Common Assembly of Asia, greeting: I should have thought that the gods themselves would see to it that such offenders should not escape. For if they had the power, they themselves would much rather punish those who refuse to worship them; but it is you who bring trouble on these persons, and accuse as the opinion of atheists that which they hold, and lay to their charge certain other things which we are unable to prove. But it would be advantageous to them that they should be thought to die for that of which they are accused, and they conquer you by being lavish of their lives rather than yield that obedience which you require of them. And regarding the earthquakes which have already happened and are now occurring, it is not seemly that you remind us of them, losing heart whenever they occur, and thus set your conduct in contrast with that of these men; for they have much greater confidence towards God than you yourselves have. And you, indeed, seem at such times to ignore the gods, and you neglect the temples, and make no recognition of the worship of God. And hence you are jealous of those who do serve Him, and persecute them to the death. Concerning such persons, some others also of the governors of provinces wrote to my most divine father; to whom he replied that they should not at all disturb such persons, unless they were found to be attempting anything against the Roman government. And to myself many have sent intimations regarding such persons, to whom I also replied in pursuance of my father's judgment. But if any one

---

[152] [Regarded as spurious.]

has a matter to bring against any person of this class, merely as such a person,[153] let the accused be acquitted of the charge, even though he should be found to be such an one; but let the accuser he [sic.] amenable to justice.

EPISTLE OF MARCUS AURELIUS TO THE SENATE IN WHICH HE TESTIFIES THAT THE CHRISTIANS WERE THE CAUSE OF HIS VICTORY.[154]

The Emperor Cæsar Marcus Aurelius Antoninus, Germanicus, Parthicus, Sarmaticus, to the People of Rome, and to the sacred Senate, greeting: I explained to you my grand design, and what advantages I gained on the confines of Germany, with much labour and suffering, in consequence of the circumstance that I was surrounded by the enemy; I myself being shut up in Carnuntum by seventy-four cohorts, nine miles off. And the enemy being at hand, the scouts pointed out to us, and our general Pompeianus showed us that there was close on us a mass of a mixed multitude of 977,000 men, which indeed we saw; and I was shut up by this vast host, having with me only a battalion composed of the first, tenth, double and marine legions. Having then examined my own position, and my host, with respect to the vast mass of barbarians and of the enemy, I quickly betook myself to prayer to the gods of my country. But being disregarded by them, I summoned those who among us go by the name of Christians. And having made inquiry, I discovered a great number and vast host of them, and raged against them, which was by no means becoming; for afterwards I learned their power. Wherefore they began the battle not by preparing weapons, nor arms, nor bugles; for

---

[153] That is, if any one accuses a Christian merely on the ground of his being a Christian.

[154] [Spurious, no doubt: but the literature of the subject is very rich. See text and notes, Milman's *Gibbon*, vol. ii. 46.]

such preparation is hateful to them, on account of the God they bear about in their conscience. Therefore it is probable that those whom we suppose to be atheists, have God as their ruling power entrenched in their conscience. For having cast themselves on the ground, they prayed not only for me, but also for the whole army as it stood, that they might be delivered from the present thirst and famine. For during five days we had got no water, because there was none; for we were in the heart of Germany, and in the enemy's territory. And simultaneously with their casting themselves on the ground, and praying to God (a God of whom I am ignorant), water poured from heaven, upon us most refreshingly cool, but upon the enemies of Rome a withering[155] hail. And immediately we recognised the presence of God following

---

[155] Literally, "fiery."

[Note I. (See capp. xxvi. and lvi.)

In 1851 I recognised this stone in the Vatican, and read it with emotion. I copied it, as follows:

"SEMONI
SANCO
DEO FIDIO
SACRUM
SEX. POMPEIUS. S. P. F. COL. MUSSIANUS.
QUTNQUENNALIS DECUR BRIDENTALIS DONTUM DEDIT."

The explanation is possibly this: Simon Magus was actually recognised as the God *Semo*. just as Barnabas and Paul were supposed to be Zeus and Hermes (Acts xiv. 12.), and were offered divine honours accordingly. Or the Samaritans may so have informed Justin on their understanding of this inscription, and with pride in the success of their countryman (Acts viii. 10), whom they had recognised" as the great power of God." See *Orelli* (No. 1860), *Insc.*, vol. i. 337.

Note II. (The Thundering Legion.)

The bas-relief on the column of Antinonine, in Rome, is a very stiking complement of the story, but an answer to prayer is not a miracle. I simply transcribe from the American Translation of Alzog's *Universal Church History* the references there given to the *Legio Fulminatrix:* "Tertull., Apol., cop. 5: Ad Scap., cap. 4: Euseb. v. 5: Greg. Nyss. Or., II in Martyr.: Oros., vii. 15: Dio Cass. Epit." Xiphilin., lib. lxxi. cap. 8; Jul. Capitol. in Marc. Antonin., cap. 24."]

75

on the prayer—a God unconquerable and indestructible. Founding upon this, then, let us pardon such as are Christians, lest they pray for and obtain such a weapon against ourselves. And I counsel that no such person be accused on the ground of his being a Christian. But if any one be found laying to the charge of a Christian that he is a Christian, I desire that it be made manifest that he who is accused as a Christian, and acknowledges that he is one, is accused of nothing else than only this, that he is a Christian; but that he who arraigns his be burned alive. And I further desire, that he who is entrusted with the government of the province shall not compel the Christian, who confesses and certifies such a matter to retract; neither shall he commit him. And I desire that these things be confirmed by a decree of the Senate. And I command this my edict to be published in the Forum of Trajan, in order that it may be read. The prefect Vitrasius Pollio will see that it be transmitted to all the provinces round about, and that no one who wishes to make use of or to possess it be hindered from obtaining a copy from the document I now publish.

THE SECOND APOLOGY OF JUSTIN

FOR THE CHRISTIANS.

ADDRESSED TO THE ROMAN SENATE.

CHAP. I.—INTRODUCTION.

Romans, the things which have recently[156] happened in your city under Urbicus,[157] and the things which are likewise being everywhere unreasonably done by the governors, have compelled me to frame this composition for your sakes, who are men of like passions, and brethren, though ye know it not, and though ye be unwilling to acknowledge it on account of your glorying in what you esteem dignities.[158] For everywhere, whoever is corrected by father, or neighbor, or child, or friend, or brother, or husband, or wife, for a fault, for being hard to move, for loving pleasure and being hard to urge to what is right (except those who have been persuaded that the unjust and intemperate shall be punished in eternal fire, but that the virtuous and those who lived like Christ shall dwell with God in a state that is free from suffering,— we mean, those who have become Christians), and the evil demons, who hate us, and who keep such men as these subject to themselves, and serving them in the capacity of judges, incite them, as rulers actuated by evil spirits, to put us to death. But that the cause of all that has taken place under Urbicus may become quite plain to you, I will relate what has been done.

---

[156] Literally, "both yesterday and the day before."
[157] [See Grabe's note on the conjecture of Valesius that this prefect was Lollius Urbicus, the historian (vol. i. p. 1. and notes, p. 1).]
[158] [He has addressed them as "Romans," because in this they gloried together,--emperor, senate, soldiers, and citizens.]

CHAP. II.—URBICUS CONDEMNS
THE CHRISTIANS TO DEATH.

A certain woman lived with an intemperate[159] husband; she herself, too, having formerly been intemperate. But when she came to the knowledge of the teachings of Christ she became sober-minded, and endeavoured to persuade her husband likewise to be temperate, citing the teaching of Christ, and assuring him that there shall be punishment in eternal fire inflicted upon those who do not live temperately and conformably to right reason. But he, continuing in the same excesses, alienated his wife from him by his actions. For she, considering it wicked to live any longer as a wife with a husband who sought in every way means of indulging in pleasure contrary to the law of nature, and in violation of what is right, wished to be divorced from him. And when she was overpersuaded by her friends, who advised her still to continue with him, in the idea that some time or other her husband might give hope of amendment, she did violence to her own feeling and remained with him. But when her husband had gone into Alexandria, and was reported to be conducting himself worse than ever, she—that she might not, by continuing in matrimonial connection with him, and by sharing his table and his bed, become a partaker also in his wickedness and impieties—gave him what you call a bill of divorce,[160] and was separated from him. But this noble husband of hers,--while he ought to have been rejoicing that those actions which formerly she unhesitatingly committed with the servants and hirelings, when she delighted in drunkenness and every vice, she had now given up, and desired that he too should give up the same,--when she had

---

[159] ἀκολασταινοντι, which word includes unchastity, as well as other forms of intemperance. [As we say, dissolute.]
[160] ᾽ρεπούδιον, i.e., "repudium," a bill of repudiation.

78

gone from him without his desire, brought an accusation against her, affirming that she was a Christian. And she presented a paper to thee, the Emperor,[161] requesting that first she be permitted to arrange her affairs, and afterwards to make her defence against the accusation, when her affairs were set in order. And this you granted. And her *quondam* husband, since he was now no longer able to prosecute her, directed his assaults against a man, Ptolemæus, whom Urbicus punished, and who had been her teacher in the Christian doctrines. And this he did in the following was. He persuaded a centurion—who had cast Ptolemæus into prison, and who was friendly to himself—to take Ptolemæus and interrogate him on this sole point: whether he were a Christian? And Ptolemæus, being a lover of truth, and not of a deceitful or false disposition, when he confessed himself to be a Christian, was bound by the centurion, and for a long time punished in the prison. And, at last, when the man[162] came to Urbicus, he was asked this one question only: whether he was a Christian? And again, being conscious of his duty, and the nobility of it through the teaching of Christ, he confessed his discipleship in the divine virtue. For he who denies anything, either denies it because he condemns the thing itself, or he shrinks from confession because he is conscious of his own unworthiness or alienation from it; neither of which cases is that of the true Christian. And when Urbicus ordered him to be led away to punishment, one Lucius, who was also himself a Christian, seeing the unreasonable judgment that had thus been given, said to Urbicus: "What is the ground of this judgment? Why have you punished this man, not as an adulterer, nor fornicator,

---

[161] [Rather, "to thee, autocrat:" a very bold apostrophe, like that of Huss to the Emperor Sigismund, which crimsoned his forehead with a blush of shame.]

[162] i.e., Ptolemæus

nor murderer, nor thief, nor robber, nor convicted of any crime at all, but who has only confessed that he is called by the name of Christian? This judgment of yours, O Urbicus, does not become the Emperor Pius, nor the philosopher, the son of Cæsar, nor the sacred senate."[163] And he said nothing else in answer to Lucius than this: "You also seem to me to be such an one." And when Lucius answered, "Most certainly I am," he again ordered him also to be led away. And he professed his thanks, knowing that he was delivered from such wicked rulers, and was going to the Father and King of the heavens. And still a third having come forward, was condemned to be punished.

CHAP. III.—JUSTIN ACCUSES CRESCENS OF IGNORANT PREJUDICE AGAINST THE CHRISTIANS.

I too, therefore, expect to be plotted against and fixed to the stake, by some of those I have named, or perhaps by Crescens, that lover of bravado and boasting;[164] for the man is not worthy of the name of philosopher who publicly bears witness against us in matters which he does not understand, saying that the Christians are atheists and impious, and doing so to win favour with the deluded mob, and to please them. For if he assails us without having read the teachings of Christ, he is thoroughly depraved, and far worse than the illiterate, who often refrain from discussing or bearing false witness about matters they do not understand. Or, if he has read them and does not understand the majesty that is in them, or, understanding it, acts thus that he may not be suspected of being such [a Christian], he is far more base and

---

[163] On this passage, see Donaldson's *Critical History*, etc., vol. ii. p. 79.
[164] Words resembling "philosopher" in sound, viz. φιλοφόφου καί φελοκομπου. [This passage is found elsewhere. See note, cap. viii., in the text preferred by Grabe.]

thoroughly depraved, being conquered by illiberal and unreasonable opinion and fear. For I would have you to know that I proposed to him certain questions on this subject, and interrogated him, and found most convincingly that he, in truth, knows nothing. And to prove that I speak the truth, I am ready, if these disputations have not been reported to you, to conduct them again in your presence. And this would be an act worthy of a prince. But if my questions and his answers have been made known to you, you are already aware that he is acquainted with none of our matters; or, if he is acquainted with them, but through fear of those who might heart him, does not dare to speak out, like Socrates, he proves himself, as I said before, no philosopher, but an opinionative man;[165] at least he does not regard that Socratic and most admirable saying: "But a man must in no wise be honoured before the truth."[166] But it is impossible for a Cynic, who makes indifference his end, to know any good but indifference.

CHAP. IV.—WHY THE CHRISTIANS DO NOT KILL THEMSELVES

But lest some one say to us, "Go then all of you and kill yourselves, and pass even now to God, and do not trouble us," I will tell you why we do not so, but why, when examined, we fearlessly confess. We have been taught that God did not make the world aimlessly, but for the sake of the human race; and we have before stated that He takes pleasure in those who imitate His properties, and is displeased with those that embrace what is worthless either in word or deed. If, then, we all kill ourselves, we shall become the cause, as far as in us lies, why no one should be born, or instructed in

---

[165] φιλόδοξος, which may mean a lover of vainglory.
[166] See Plato, *Rep.*, p. 595.

the divine doctrines, or even why the human race should not exist; and we shall, if we so act, be ourselves acting in opposition to the will of God. But when we are examined, we make no denial, because we are not conscious of any evil, but count it impious not to speak the truth in all things, which also we know is pleasing to God, and because we are also now very desirous to deliver you from an unjust prejudice.

CHAP. V.—HOW THE ANGELS TRANSGRESSED.

But if this idea take possession of some one, that if we acknowledge God as our helper, we should not, as we say, be oppressed and persecuted by the wicked; this, too, I will solve. God, when He had made the whole world, and subjected things earthly to man, and arranged the heavenly elements for the increase of fruits and rotation of the seasons, and appointed this divine law—for these things also He evidently made for man—committed the care of men and of all things under heaven to angels transgressed this appointment, and were captivated by love of women, and begat children who are those that are called demons; and besides they afterwards subdued the human race to themselves, partly by magical writings, and partly by fears and the punishments they occasioned, and partly by teaching them to offer sacrifices, and incense, and libations, of which things they stood in need after they were enslaved by lustful passions; and among men they sowed murders, wars, adulteries, intemperate deeds, and all wickedness. Whence also the poets and mythologists, not knowing that it was the angels and those demons who had been begotten by them that did these things to men, and women, and cities, and nations, which they related, ascribed them to god himself, and to those who were accounted to be his very offspring, and to the offspring of those who were called his brothers, Neptune and Pluto, and to the children again of these their offspring. For whatever name each of the angels had given to himself and his children, by that name they called them.

CHAP. VI.—NAMES OF GOD AND OF CHRIST, THEIR MEANING AND POWER.

But to the Father of all, who is unbegotten, there is no name given. For by whatever name He be called, He has as His elder the person who gives Him the name. But these words, Father, and God, and Creator, and Lord, and Master, are not names, but appellations derived from His good deeds and functions. And His Son, who alone is properly called Son, the Word, who also was with Him and was begotten before the works, when at first He created and arranged all things by Him, is called Christ, in reference to His being anointed and God's ordering all things through Him; this name itself also containing an unknown significance; as also the appellation "God" is not a name, but an opinion implanted in the nature of men of a thing that can hardly be explained. But "Jesus," His name as man and Saviour, has also significance. For He was made man also, as we before said, having been conceived according to the will of God the Father, for the sake of believing men, and for the destruction of the demons. And now you can learn this from what is under your own observation. For numberless demoniacs throughout the whole world, and in your city, many of our Christian men exorcising them in the name of Jesus Christ, who was crucified under Pontius Pilate, have healed and do heal, rendering helpless and driving the possessing devils out of the men, though they could not be cured by all the other exorcists, and those who used incantations and drugs.

CHAP. VII.—THE WORLD PRESERVED FOR THE SAKE OF CHRISTIANS. MAN'S RESPONSIBILITY.

Wherefore God delays causing the confusion and destruction of the whole world, by which the wicked angels and demons and men shall cease to exist, because of the seed of the Christians, who know that they are the cause of preservation in nature.[167] Since, if it were not so, it would not have been possible for you to do these things, and to be impelled by evil spirits; but the fire of judgment would descend and utterly dissolve all things, even as formerly the flood left no one but him only with his family who is by us called Noah, and by you Deucalion, from whom again such vast numbers have sprung, some of them evil and others good. For so we say that there will be the conflagration, but not as the Stoics, according to their doctrine of all things being changed into one another, which seems most degrading. But neither do we affirm that it is by fate that men do what they do, or suffer what they suffer, but that each man by free choice acts rightly or sins; and that it is by the influence of the wicked demons that earnest men, such as Socrates and the like, suffer persecution and are in bonds, while Sardanapalus, Epicurus, and the like, seem to be blessed in abundance and glory. The Stoics, not observing this, maintained that all things take place according to the necessity of fate. But since God in the beginning made the race of angels and men with free-will, they will justly suffer in eternal fire the punishment of whatever sins they have committed. And this is the nature of all that is made, to be capable of vice and virtue. For neither would any of them be praiseworthy unless there were power to turn to both [virtue and vice]. And this also is shown by those men everywhere

---

[167] This is Dr. Donaldson's rendering of a clause on which the editors differ both as to reading and rendering.

84

who have made laws and philosophized according to right reason, by their prescribing to do some things and refrain from others. Even the Stoic philosophers, in their doctrine of morals, steadily honour the same things, so that it is evident that they are not very felicitous in what they say about principles and incorporeal things. For if they say that human actions come to pass by fate, they will maintain either that God is nothing else than the things which are ever turning, and altering, and dissolving into the same things, and will appear to have had a comprehension only of things that are destructible, and to have looked on God Himself as emerging both in part and in whole in every wickedness;[168] or that neither vice nor virtue is anything; which is contrary to every sound idea, reason, and sense.

CHAP. VIII.—ALL HAVE BEEN HATED IN WHOM THE WORD HAS DWELT.

And those of the Stoic school—since, so far as their moral teaching went, they were admirable, as were also the poets in some particulars, on account of the seed of reason [the Logos] implanted in every race of men—were, we know, hated and put to death,--Heraclitus for instance, and, among those of our own time, Musonius and others. For, as we intimated, the devils have always effected, that all those who anyhow live a reasonable and earnest life, and shun vice, be hated. And it is nothing wonderful; if the devils are proved to cause those to be much worse hated who live not according to a part only of the word diffused [among men], but by the knowledge and contemplation of the whole Word, which is Christ. And they, having been shut up in eternal fire, shall suffer their just punishment and penalty. For if they are even

---

[168] Literally, "becoming (γινόμενον) both through the parts and through the whole in every wickedness.

now overthrown by men through the name of Jesus Christ, this is an intimation of the punishment in eternal fire which is to be inflicted on themselves and those who serve them. For thus did both all the prophets foretell, and our own teacher Jesus teach.[169]

CHAP. IX.—ETERNAL PUNISHMENT NOT A MERE THREAT.

And that no one may say what is said by those who are deemed philosophers, that our assertions that the wicked are punished in eternal fire are big words and bugbears, and that we wish men to live virtuously through fear, and not because such a life is good and pleasant; I will briefly reply to this, that if this be not so, God does not exist; or, if He exists, He cares not for men, and neither virtue nor vice is anything, and, as we said before, lawgivers unjustly punish those who transgress good commandments. But since these are not unjust, and their Father teaches them by the word to do the same things as Himself, they who agree with them are not unjust. And if one object that the laws of men are diverse, and say that with some, one thing is considered good, another evil, while with others what seemed bad to the former is esteemed good, and what seemed good is esteemed bad, let him listen to what we say to this. We know that the wicked angels appointed laws conformable to their own wickedness, in which the men who are like them delight; and the right Reason,[170] when He came, proved that not all opinions nor all doctrines are good, but that some are evil, while others are good. Wherefore, I will declare the same and similar things to such men as these, and, if need be, they

---

[169] [Here, in Grabe's text, comes the passage about Crescens.]

[170] These words can be taken of the Logos as well as of the right reason diffused among men by Him.

shall be spoken of more at large. But at present I return to the subject.

CHAP. X.—CHRIST COMPARED WITH SOCRATES.

Our doctrines, then appear to be greater than all human teaching; because Christ, who appeared for our sakes, became the whole rational being, both body, and reason, and soul. For whatever either lawgivers, or philosophers uttered well, they elaborated by finding and contemplating some part of the Word. But since they did not know the whole of the Word, which is Christ, they often contradicted themselves. And those who by human birth were more ancient than Christ, when they attempted to consider and prove things by reason, were brought before the tribunals as impious persons and busybodies. And Socrates, who was more zealous in this direction than all of them, was accused of the very same crimes as ourselves. For they said that he was introducing new divinities, and did not consider those to be gods whom the state recognised. But he cast out from the state both Homer[171] and the rest of the poets, and taught men to reject the wicked demons and those who did the things which the poets related; and he exhorted them to become acquainted with the God who was to them unknown, by means of the investigation of reason, saying, "That it is neither easy to find the Father and Maker of all, nor, having found Him, is it safe to declare Him to all."[172] But these things our Christ did through His own power. For no one trusted in Socrates so as to die for this doctrine, but in Christ, who was partially known even by Socrates (for He was and is the Word who is in every man, and who foretold the things that were to come

---

[171] Plato, *Rep.*, x. c. i. p. 525.
[172] Plat., *Timæus*, p. 28. C. (but "possible," and not "safe," is the word used by Plato).

to pass both through the prophets and in His own person when He was made of like passions, and taught these things), not only philosophers and scholars believed, but also artisans and people entirely uneducated, despising both glory, and fear, and death; since He is a power of the ineffable Father, and not the mere instrument of human reason.[173]

CHAP. XI.—HOW CHRISTIANS VIEW DEATH.

But neither should we be put to death, nor would wicked men and devils be more powerful than we, were not death a debt due by every man that is born. Wherefore we give thanks when we pay this debt. And we judge it right and opportune to tell here, for the sake of Crescens and those who rave as he does, what is related by Xenophon. Hercules, says Xenophon, coming to a place where three ways met, found Virtue and Vice, who appeared to him in the form of women: Vice, in a luxurious dress, and with a seductive expression rendered blooming by such ornaments, and her eyes of a quickly melting tenderness,[174] said to Hercules that if he would follow her, she would always enable him to pass his life in pleasure and adorned with the most graceful ornaments, such as were then upon her own person; and Virtue, who was of squalid look and dress, said, But if you obey me, you shall adorn yourself not with ornament nor beauty that passes away and perishes, but with everlasting and precious graces. And we are persuaded that every one who flees those things that seem to be good, and follows hard after what are reckoned difficult and strange, enters into blessedness. For Vice, when by imitation of what is

---

[173] [Certainly the author of this chapter, and others like it, cannot be accused of a feeble rhetoric.]

[174] Another reading is πρός τάς ὄψεις, referring to the eyes of the beholder: and which may be rendered, "speedily fascinating to the sight."

incorruptible (for what is really incorruptible she neither has nor can produce) she has thrown around her own actions, as a disguise, the properties of Virtue, and qualities which are really excellent, leads captive earthly-minded men, attaching to Virtue her own evil properties. But those who understood the excellences which belong to that which is real, are also uncorrupt in virtue. And this every sensible person ought to think both of Christians and of the athletes, and of those who did what the poets relate of the so-called gods, concluding as much from our contempt of death, even when it could be escaped.[175]

CHAP. XII.—CHRISTIANS PROVED INNOCENT BY THEIR CONTEMPT OF DEATH.

For I myself, too, when I was delighting in the doctrines of Plato, and heard the Christians slandered, and saw them fearless of death, and of all other things which are counted fearful, perceived that it was impossible that they could be living in wickedness and pleasure. For what sensual or intemperate man, or who that counts it good to feast on human flesh,[176] could welcome death that he might be deprived of his enjoyments, and would not rather continue always the present life, and attempt to escape the observation of the rulers; and much less would he denounce himself when the consequence would be death? This also the wicked demons have now caused to be done by evil men. For having put some to death on account of the accusations falsely brought against us, they also dragged to the torture our domestics, either children or weak women, and by dreadful torments forced them to admit those fabulous actions which

---

[175] Καί φευκτοῦ θανάτου may also be rendered, "even of death *which men flee from.*"

[176] Alluding to the common accusation against the Christians.

they themselves openly perpetrate; about which we are the less concerned, because none of these actions are really ours, and we have the unbegotten and ineffable God as witness both of our thoughts and deeds. For why did we not even publicly profess that these were the things which we esteemed good, and prove that these are the divine philosophy, saying that the mysteries of Saturn are performed when we slay a man, and that when we drink our fill of blood, as it is said we do, we are doing what you do before that idol you honour, and on which you sprinkle the blood not only of irrational animals, but also of men, making a libation of the blood of the slain by the hand of the most illustrious and noble man among you? And imitating Jupiter and the other gods in sodomy and shameless intercourse with a woman, might we not bring as our apology the writings of Epicurus and the poets? But because we persuade men to avoid such instruction, and all who practise them and imitate such examples, as now in this discourse we have striven to persuade you, we are assailed in every kind of way. But we are not concerned, since we know that god is a just observer of all. But would that even now some one would mount a lofty rostrum, and shout with a loud voice,[177] "Be ashamed, be ashamed, ye who charge the guiltless with those deeds which yourselves openly commit, and ascribe things which apply to yourselves and to your gods to those who have not even the slightest sympathy with them. Be ye converted; become wise."

---

[177] Literally, "with tragic voice,"—the loud voice in which the Greek tragedies were recited through the *mask* [*persona*].

CHAP. XIII.—HOW THE
WORD HAS BEEN IN ALL MEN.

For I myself, when I discovered the wicked disguise which the evil spirits had thrown around the divine doctrines of the Christians, to turn aside others from joining them, laughed both at those who framed these falsehoods, and at the disguise itself, and at popular opinion; and I confess that I both boast and with all my strength strive to be found a Christian; not because the teachings of Plato are different from those of Christ, but because they are not in all respects similar, as neither are those of the others, Stoics, and poets, and historians. For each man spoke well in proportion to the share he had of the spermatic word,[178] seeing what was related to it. but they who contradict themselves on the more important points appear not to have possessed the heavenly[179] wisdom, and the knowledge which cannot be spoken against. Whatever things were rightly said among all men, are the property of us Christians. For next to God, we worship and love the Word who is from the unbegotten and ineffable God, since also He became man for our sakes, that, becoming a partaker of our sufferings, He might also bring us healing. For all the writers were able to see realities darkly through the sowing of the implanted word that was in them. For the seed and imitation imparted according to capacity is one thing, and quite another is the thing itself, of which there is the participation and imitation according to the grace which is from Him.

---

[178] The word disseminated among men. [St. James i. 21.]
[179] Literally, dimly seen at a distance.

CHAP. XIV.—JUSTIN PRAYS
THAT THIS APPEAL BE PUBLISHED.

And we therefore pray you to publish this little book, appending what you think right, that our opinions may be known to others, and that these persons may have a fair chance of being freed from erroneous notions and ignorance of good, who by their own fault are become subject to punishment; that so these things may be published to men, because it is in the nature of man to know good and evil; and by their condemning us, whom they do not understand, for actions which they say are wicked, and by delighting in the gods who did such things, and even now require similar actions from men, and by inflicting on us death or bonds or some other such punishment, as if we were guilty of these things, they condemn themselves, so that there is no need of other judges.

CHAP. XV.—CONCLUSION.

And I despised the wicked and deceitful doctrine of Simon[180] of my own nation. And if you give this book your authority, we will expose him before all, that, if possible, they may be converted. For this end alone did we compose this treatise. And our doctrines are not shameful, according to a sober judgment, but are indeed more lofty than all human philosophy; and if not so, they are at least unlike the doctrines of the Sotadists, and Philænidians, and Dancers, and Epicureans, and such other teachings of the poets, which all are allowed to acquaint themselves with, both as acted and as written. And henceforth we shall be silent, having

---

[180] [Simon Magus appears to be one with whom Justin is perfectly familiar, and hence we are not to conclude rashly that he blundered as to the divine honours rendered to him as the Sabine God.]

done as much as we could, and having added the prayer that all men everywhere may be counted worthy of the truth. And would that you also in a manner becoming piety and philosophy,[181] would for your own sakes judge justly!

---

[181] [Another apostrophe, and a home thrust for "Pius the philosopher" and emperor.]

INDEX

95

www.ingramcontent.com/pod-product-compliance
Lightning Source LLC
Chambersburg PA
CBHW070827100426
42813CB00003B/513